DARKNESS

DARKNESS

WHERE DOES IT COME FROM?

BARBARA M. HARDIE

Crystal Clear Publishing
Tolland, Massachusetts
email: Barbara@angelconnections.com
www.angelconnections.com

Cover Artwork: Sue Muldoon Images, LLC
www.suemuldoonimages.com
Layout and Printing: Paradise Copies, Inc., Northampton, MA
Editor: JoAnn Deck

ISBN: 978-0-9837533-2-2
First Printing – October 2015

Printed in the United States of America

Disclaimer:

Darkness: Where Does It Come From? may contain information
that opposes traditional beliefs. This is not meant to offend anyone.
It is provided from the author's personal experiences and spiritual
perspective. The author is not a medical practitioner and in no way
is providing medical advice or diagnosis, and therefore, strongly
encourages anyone dealing with health issues to seek professional help.
The information provided is strictly for information purpose only and
the author is not responsible for any actions taken by the reader.

DEDICATION

It is with a great deal of Love & Light that I dedicate *Darkness: Where Does It Come From?* to all the wonderful Beings of Light, who have assisted me in bringing this book into reality. There were times when I wasn't sure I was going to complete it.

I would like to express my heartfelt appreciation and thanks to:

Jesus/Sananda – for all of His wonderful messages; for overseeing the project and making the connections behind the scenes for the channeled messages; and for guiding me as to what was necessary to be included. He was a HUGE contributor.

Jonathan (My Master Guide) – who has been with me daily to help in any way he could. He is my "rock."

Dr. Joshua David Stone – was my teacher/mentor regarding Ascension and he has been instrumental in connecting me with Kuthumi, Sanat Kumara and Serapis Bey.

Samuel – was the first to come forward with his message for this book and I loved it.

Sanat Kumara – I was very pleased to have Sanat Kumara come forward as I had connected with him many years ago, but he did not give his name, only that he was from Venus. I thought it was pretty cool to connect with someone from Venus during my early days of meditation.

Serapis Bey – I had known of Serapis Bey through Dr. Joshua David Stone's books and classes so I was honored to receive a message from him.

Kuthumi – again I knew of Kuthumi through Dr. Joshua David Stone, but have never had the pleasure of connecting directly with him. I hope he will have occasion to connect with me again.

The Arcturians – I have been working with the Arcturians for approximately 15 years and they are absolutely wonderful Souls very anxious to help humanity with our journey on Earth.

Universal Mother God – I was so thrilled and honored and I thank Mother God for the important message She provided for humanity.

Also, I would especially like to thank the following celebrities for coming forward with their messages. It was a real honor and pleasure to be able to communicate with them:

Robin Williams

John Lennon

Michael Jackson
President John F. Kennedy
John F. Kennedy, Jr.
Marilyn Monroe
Princess Diana

I feel I am truly blessed to be able to communicate with Spirit and bring their messages forward.

Darkness:
Where Does It Come From?

TABLE OF CONTENTS

ACKNOWLEDGMENTS

First of all, I would like to acknowledge and thank all the governmental, political, and military leaders who are NOT part of the Shadow Government, Illuminati, or other Secret Societies referred to in *Darkness: Where Does It Come From?* for their loyal and dedicated service.

While *Darkness: Where Does It Come From?* paints a pretty ugly picture of what is going on behind the scenes on Planet Earth, I know that the majority of individuals associated with the world governments are doing a very good and honest job. They most likely are unaware of the ultimate goal of a One World Government and the plan of domination or destruction of Earth.

I also have a great deal of Faith and Trust in the Beings of Light that they will not only lead us out of darkness, but will provide assistance in whatever we need to complete our mission of connecting Heaven and Earth.

God Bless Humanity!

Introduction

DARKNESS: WHERE DOES IT COME FROM?

In the fall of 2013, I was scheduled to be the minister for church service. I asked my Guides to help me choose a new subject to talk about. Something I had not already talked about in the past. I forgot about the rule "be careful what you ask for." My Spiritual Helpers guided me to the topic of "darkness."

I spoke briefly on the subject at church service the following Sunday, and during social hour afterwards several individuals indicated that they felt "darkness" was the subject of my next book. Unfortunately, I, too, had that same feeling.

Spirit confirmed our suspicions, but that was it. Not having any idea where to start on this subject, I asked Spirit to please lead me in the right direction so that I could research the subject. They provided me with an outline for the book and I began my research.

This outline included many well-known individuals (now in Spirit) who would come forward and provide me with messages for the book. Several of the Light Beings would also be coming forward to provide their messages. Therefore, the information contained in this book is what the Beings of Light want to bring to our attention at this time.

I thought it was strange that I should write a book on this topic. There are so many others much more knowledgeable than I am on this subject. I felt like a fish out of water (and I'm a Pisces). I thought that if someone such as an ex-President or another world leader wrote a book on this subject, it would carry more weight as they would have had firsthand knowledge/experience of operating under the umbrella of darkness.

I am definitely NOT an expert on darkness – at least not in this lifetime. Not sure what I experienced in my other lifetimes in order for me to be an author on the subject of darkness in this lifetime. I had made an agreement while on the Other Side that, in this lifetime, I would write a series of books in order to help humanity awaken to what our purpose is for being in human form.

I have done some basic research, but had no idea the massive scope of this subject. It was like a snowball. One thing led to another, then another, and yet another and it kept on going. Since it was Jesus/Sananda who guided me to write on this subject, I am taking direction from Him regarding what should be included in order to assist humanity in knowing that the "wool" has been pulled over our eyes far too long.

Therefore, with the help of Jesus/Sananda and many other Angelic Light Beings, I have written *Darkness: Where Does It Come From?* I still do not consider myself an expert on the subject, nor do I want to be. However, what I can say is that I do not view darkness as something to fear, but something to embrace, to release, and to let go of it.

The subject of darkness is so vast that to do it justice one would need to write an entire set of encyclopedia. However, I have been guided by many Light Beings who have included what they feel is important for humanity to know at this time.

So many individuals, including myself earlier in this lifetime, found it very comforting to blame others for our problems. It seems so much easier to deal with the struggles of life if we believe that we had nothing to do with causing them. In fact, the complete opposite is true. The answers to our challenges of life reside within our Soul Plan/Contract/Blueprint. Life is much easier if we look within to resolve quickly and easily whatever is making us uncomfortable.

One thing I have learned over the years with working/communicating with the Light Beings is that their spiritual perspective is totally different than the human Third

Dimensional perspective – our reality/illusion. Therefore, I ask that you please keep an open mind while reading *Darkness: Where Does It Come From?* The Beings of Light are looking at darkness as a necessary experience to help us in making our Free Will decisions for growth purposes and return to the Light. It is part of the Plan/Contract for humanity.

First, we will take a look at the reason why, not only the Planet was created, but also why humanity was created.

Next, we will move on to Lucifer's purpose. It is extremely difficult for a very high level spiritual being to be encased in a human/physical body. However, Lucifer took on this challenge for the GOOD of humanity. Unfortunately, other outside influences/sources interfered with his carrying out the Plan to its full potential. His reign has ended. But some of his followers are still fighting the war of Good vs. Evil.

Evil is just the opposite of Good so it is important to note that humans can fluctuate back and forth between the two opposites at any given moment. Our spiritual partners do not look at humanity as "evil." They see wonderful bright shining Souls who are serving a purpose – all working toward the good of humanity. Both good and evil will blend together and equal out for the good. Many times when humans "appear" to act out in a negative way, it is in fact for the good, even though it does not seem so at the time of the event.

Then we will look at the purpose, importance, and necessity for duality and why it is part of our Free Will experience.

The next section will give us a deeper study of darkness, the Dark Night of the Soul, and how to overcome darkness. I will give you my best guidance from my research and from my Spiritual Helpers.

The Secret Societies play a major role in the darkness on Earth so a large section will be devoted to their activities. This includes the Illuminati, the Committee of 300, The Bilderberg Group, and the Shadow Government.

Also, the Dark Reptilians and Greys (entities not of this world) play an even greater role on Earth as they rule the Secret Societies and governments and have taken control of Earth. Again, I encourage you to keep an open mind in reading all of these sections.

Remember that our experiences on Earth are part of an "Experiment." View it as a long running Hollywood movie and each of us has a part to play. Know that at the end of this movie, it will have a happy ending, when we (all of humanity) will be able to stand up and take a bow as we receive a standing ovation from our Heavenly Helpers.

Humanity is a species that is destined to be Gods and are now in training for this position. It almost seems impossible that we, as a human being, could ever be a God. Not all will reach this level in this lifetime, however, many will.

We will need much guidance from the Other Side.

This is why it is important for us to connect with our Heavenly Helpers. Life becomes much easier once we allow the guidance, which we included in our Life Plan, to assist our journey here on Earth.

If we take advantage of the assistance these wonderful Light Beings are so graciously willing to provide us, we will have no problem reaching our full potential, first as Ascended Masters, then moving up to combine our energy with our God Self.

We all have a dark or so-called shadow side and depending upon our spiritual growth and the circumstances placed before us, our Free Will decisions determine whether we move forward on our path or if we regress. At a certain time, we need to make the decision which path we want to take – that of good or that of evil.

As we grow spiritually, the decision becomes much easier as we will find that the good/positive path feels so much better than the bad/negative path. Life becomes joyful – free of challenges. The opposite holds true for those who choose the negative path. They feel angry, revengeful, hopeless, and a sense that life is filled with problems.

Even though we all have a combination of Light and Dark energies, it is our responsibility to overcome the negative/Dark with positive/Light experiences to reach the middle. This is what is referred to as balance. Being in human form, we would unlikely be able to dissolve the dark completely.

To overcome the negative challenges which surround us on a daily basis, we will not need to start a world war or have destructive weapons. We can have our own "secret" weapon – prayer meetings to call upon the Forces of Light to step in and help us even more than they have been able to do so far.

Our Free Will has put up boundaries regarding the amount of help the Beings of Light are able to provide. However, if we ask they can step in and provide us with additional assistance. This problem of darkness has become too massive for us to handle on our own without intervention from the Beings of Light. Remember "Ask and You Shall Receive" is very important at this particular time in Earth's history.

The purpose of this book is to bring awareness as to why Planet Earth was created and, more importantly, to bring to light the activities of the Dark Ones and their ultimate goal of world domination or destruction, and finally, what we (humanity) need to do in order to fulfill our mission of Creating Heaven on Earth.

We are receiving a great deal of help from those who came before us. While we may think we cannot do anything, we absolutely can. We have a "silent weapon" called PRAYER. We can pray individually or we can pray in groups for World Peace. The more we increase our Light quotient, the higher the Planet will rise in vibration as well.

Humanity is opening its awareness of the mistakes we

have made in the past and that it is time to take our power back by voicing our opinions about what is happening with our lawmakers. It is time that we revert back to the original Constitution that the forefathers of this country established for our benefit. The Constitution has been deliberately changed over the years to serve the "Shadow Government's" needs, and little by little we went down under and I don't mean to Australia. Down under in our own homeland.

You will find that from the spiritual perspective Lucifer had a Divine purpose in the Great Experiment, and he is portrayed as a "good" guy. This may anger or even infuriate many readers. Please know that this is not my intention. Keep in mind and look at what Spirit has to say about the TRUTH of Lucifer's mission before making judgment.

I didn't want to research the history of Lucifer as I felt it would open the door for him to come to me and bring his darkness into my life. I had worked so hard to release as much negativity within me as possible and replace it with Light that I didn't want to regress even for a moment.

But how can you write a book about darkness and not include Lucifer? So I decided to begin my research. During my initial days of research, I think it was my "fear," my imagination, because I felt that my energy had gone down a notch or two and that little negative annoying things were starting to pop up in my life. I was sure this was a result of spending my days focusing on the subject of darkness.

I am a firm believer that your thoughts create your

reality. So, during meditation, I reached up to God and said that I was not comfortable writing this book I had been guided to write.

Mother Mary came forward and assured me that no harm would befall me or anyone else as a result of my mission. She suggested that I call upon my Guides of Light to be with me as I did my research and I would be fine. This proved to be true. From that point forward, I released my fear and also took on the same positive perspective about Lucifer's mission as Spirit had expressed. He was a God-created Light Being who had a mission and was playing that role as intended.

It is the same as we experience in games of sport. There are two teams which play the same game, but only one team emerges the winner. But that does not mean that we only love the players on the winning team. We still love the players on the losing team. We support, encourage, and cheer them on and hope that they will emerge winners during the next game.

The "Game of Life" for humans is similar. The players on one team appear to be "winners," but that does not mean that we have to hate the ones who are playing on the other team. Eventually we will all be on the same team. It's just that we have to finish the game first. The only thing we are assured of is that Light will definitely win. This is God's Plan and so it is already done.

Those who chose to play on the darkness team have been informed that they lost the Game, but some are not willing to believe this for their leader told them they would be the winners. Therefore, they are continuing with their dark activities. However, they no longer have a leader here on Earth to follow so we should be witnessing signs of dark activities fading from our experiences. What will remain will be the dark thought forms which all of humanity are contributing to the overall universal energy source. We can eliminate these thought forms by bringing Light to the Planet for their dissolution. This can be done through prayer, through visualizing a net of White Light enveloping the darkness, and also by keeping our thoughts as clean and positive as possible.

In order to finish on a positive note, I have included a section on what the Heavenly Helpers are doing to protect us and Planet Earth during these difficult times. Also included is a section with channeled messages from the Light Beings regarding the subject of darkness. In addition to this section, there are messages from individuals in the Spirit World included throughout the book.

We have arrived in the Golden Age so think positive and KNOW that you are on your path practicing to be a God here on Earth, by creating Heaven on Earth as your reality through your thoughts, words, actions, and feelings!

While there is much more information available regarding darkness, this is just a brief overview of what we need to be conscious of and the steps we can take in order to bring about Peace and Heaven on Earth.

PART I

PURPOSE OF EARTH AND HUMANITY

Chapter 1

PURPOSE OF EARTH & HUMANITY

Once upon a time there was an entity known as Source/Creator of All That Is. "He" created many, many planets, galaxies, and universes. Eventually "He" grew tired of doing everything by himself so He created some very high level Light Beings and called them Gods.

Each of these Gods headed up one of the Universes created by Source/Creator. Then Source/Creator passed on to these Gods the ability to be able to create their own planets, galaxies, and universes. In so doing, they became co-creators with Source.

This was great fun. However, the Gods also wanted to pass their abilities onto others. It was decided to create a planet where Souls from the higher realms could descend into the lower planes, and as a result of making their own

Free Will decisions, would go through the process of Awakening and Ascension and evolve to the level of Ascended Master.

As Ascended Masters they would not have to return to Earth, unless they wanted to in order to help other Soul Group members to reach the Ascended Master vibrational level. As Ascended Masters they could remain on the Other Side and start the process of becoming Gods and creating their own planets, galaxies, and universes.

AN EXAMPLE OF OUR MISSION

I would like to share an example of our mission in becoming a God. A friend of mine lost her son quite unexpectedly. Upon connecting with his energy after his passing, he indicated that it was his time. His contract for being on Earth was up as he had reached the Ascended Master vibration and he had important things to do on the Other Side. His mother had the ability to communicate with him and when she asked him what he was doing, he replied that he was in the process of learning how to create a planet. He told her, if they created something and did not like the outcome, all they had to do was dissolve it and do it over.

This is a first step (on the Other Side) to becoming a God. He finished his practice work on Earth and it was time for him to do the real work in the Heavenly Realm. This is a reminder that all of humanity has the ability to create our own reality while on Earth. We do this through our thoughts, words, actions, and feelings. So if we do not like what has been created in our life, we have the power to change our circumstances through our thoughts, words, actions, and feelings and I will add prayer to this list as well, especially when it comes to changing darkness into Light. If you think there is nothing you can do, you need to change your thinking and reach up to your Heavenly Helpers. When we combine our thoughts with the Heavenly Light Beings, anything/everything IS possible!

We, as humans, have this ability on Earth while we are in training. Our thoughts, words, actions, and feelings create our reality so if we don't like what is happening in our life, we can change it by changing our thoughts, words, actions, and feelings to something more positive – something that would make life more pleasurable.

While we are on the Other Side in our Spirit bodies, everything is blissful. We do not have to deal with challenges or problems. Therefore, Planet Earth was created as the Great Experiment to see how Souls would react to the symptoms of duality. Darkness/Duality is not something we were exposed to in the Heavenly Realm.

THE GIFT OF FREE WILL

The God in charge of Planet Earth decided that the human occupants of Earth would have the gift of Free Will. How we reacted to certain situations/circumstances in our life would determine whether we grew spiritually or stayed stuck in a lower vibration. If we reacted in a neutral or positive manner, it meant that we had risen above the challenge.

When we do not allow anger, depression or other negative energies to step in, we grow to a higher vibration.

Planet Earth was created in the Third Dimension vibration – referred to as the lower astral plane. As Souls, we resided in the Seventh Dimension. Coming down from the Seventh Dimension to the Third Dimension was a very challenging experience for many humans, especially since we lost our memory/knowledge of who we were while in the Seventh Dimension.

We were not cast out of Heaven and into Hell (Earth) because we went against God. Those of us who chose the Human experience (the Great Experiment) volunteered for this mission. We are working in tandem with God to fulfill a very important yet difficult mission – to bring a Planet from a low vibration up to a higher vibration and actually connect Heaven and Earth together as ONE. It's time for us to finally complete this wonderful mission. It will be worth whatever pain and suffering we had to endure during many lifetimes to be able to do something that has never been done before.

Through the process of reincarnation, we have a choice as to whether or not we return to Earth lifetime after lifetime. We do not have to be here and endure the struggles we have been subjected to over many lifetimes. Therefore, while it appears that we are "victims," truly we are not – we are Gods in training!

CREATING PEACE AND HEAVEN ON EARTH

Planet Earth is a temporary home for humanity until we fulfill our mission of Creating Peace and Heaven on Earth.

Planet Earth is giving humanity an opportunity to grow to a certain vibrational level of Light in order to become co-creators with God as God is a co-creator with Source.

This Great Experiment we are experiencing was not destined to last forever. There was a time-frame involved to complete our mission. That timeframe is NOW! The experience of darkness/duality has reached its expiration date; however, it will probably take some time before it is eliminated completely. Be patient. We are on the right path – the path to fulfilling our mission of Creating Heaven on Earth.

Chapter 2

LUCIFER'S PURPOSE

Lucifer is a high-level, God-created Being of Light who took on the role of darkness (opposite of Light) for Earth's Great Experiment. He made a very important sacrifice for humanity's mission on Earth – more so than we will ever know.

WHAT WAS LUCIFER'S PURPOSE?

Lucifer came onto Earth with full consciousness of what his purpose was. However, he decided not to be connected with the Angels or Spirit Guides as humans could access during their journey on Earth. He did keep the connection with his Twin Flame (Hope), Archangel Gabriel, as well as Jesus, and other members of his Council in order to review progress on Earth.

Lucifer's original purpose was to teach the opposite of what we experienced in the higher dimensions – separation from God, instead of Oneness with God. Being an individual, alone, and with the assistance of the Ego Self, we could manage very nicely on our own. Humans did not need to believe in an invisible outside source. While it was perceived as a Free Will decision to separate ourselves from God, in fact, it was part of the original plan for humanity during the Great Experiment of Life on Earth.

His mission was NOT evil, just different – the opposite of Light, which is dark. In the beginning, Lucifer was not successful in his efforts as he carried too much Light in his Soul. People did not believe his teachings.

VEIL OF FORGETFULNESS

Eventually, Lucifer was able to increase the number of followers by preaching that they did not need God; that they could survive on their own. When humans were experiencing the challenges that life on Earth has to offer, Lucifer was able to recruit a great number of followers due to the veil of forgetfulness. We did not remember that we were God-created Beings of Light and could reach up and connect with our Heavenly Helpers to receive the help we needed. We only knew of our human existence and the suffering we had to endure.

GIFTS OF LUCIFER

Humanity did fall victim to darkness through the vibrations of fear, greed, poverty consciousness, lust, pride, insecurity, and especially through major extraterrestrial influences.

FEAR & GREED

Lucifer existed under the umbrella of FEAR. His specialty was to create fear and take what belonged to someone else as opposed to earning or attaining things that would be rightfully his. Because this was so prevalent on Earth (taking what belonged to others and making it your own), it was perceived that owning material possessions was evil.

POVERTY CONSCIOUSNESS

On the other hand, God wanted abundance for all of His children, and through our connection with Him, we could obtain our heart's desires legally. Unfortunately, Lucifer created poverty consciousness in the humans following the path of Light.

Poverty consciousness is beginning to lift somewhat, but is still engrained in many who believe it is WRONG to ask God for what they want or need. Personally, I have gotten over the wrongness of asking God for what I want/need, and life is so much better when you are not dealing with lack from month to month.

There is absolutely nothing wrong with living a prosperous life. It is how one goes about attaining their wealth that is important. If we use Light methods it is fine. If we use illegal/dark methods then we have a spiritual price to pay called Karma.

ORIGINAL SIN/LUST

Lucifer enticed Eve to eat the forbidden fruit from the

Tree of Knowledge in the Garden of Eden. I often wondered how eating a healthy apple could be considered evil. Well, it wasn't the fruit at all. It was Lucifer's lustful relationship with Eve in the Garden of Eden (what we would consider an affair by today's verbiage) which created the so-called original sin, and it has followed human history right up to the present day. The type of love-making that exists today is (for the most part) that created by Lucifer (lustful), not God (a sacred expression of love).

INSECURITY

Another "gift" Lucifer gave humanity was insecurity. He was pretending to be someone he was not – God! God is Love and Light, not Darkness. Until humanity can release and let go of their insecurities and fears established during their incarnations on Earth, evil will still exist. The higher the level of spiritual vibration we are able to attain, the easier it is for us to let go of these negative energies we do not need. When I am talking with people and hear them say "I am afraid of this," or "I fear that," it makes me very uncomfortable. I usually say "you have nothing to fear or be afraid of."

REPTILIAN INFLUENCE

At one point, Lucifer had absolutely NO effect on humanity as the Reptilians were in complete control. The Reptilians are not of this world. They have taken over control of Earth and are spreading darkness across the planet through our world leaders and military forces.

Therefore, in order to carry out his mission, Lucifer decided to reincarnate into the Reptilian-controlled families and fight them with deception – making them believe he was one of them (not a Light Being). They naturally were skeptical at first, but Lucifer demonstrated very powerful qualities, such as breathing out fire and causing his eyes to become red when angry. These qualities impressed the Reptilians as they were not able to perform such acts to show their anger. So they accepted him for what he could do to help them with their cause of spreading darkness in order to control humanity. In other words, Lucifer, as a Light Being, had to infiltrate the ranks of the real dark ETs in order to fulfill his mission on Earth.

LUCIFER'S DUAL PURPOSES

Keep in mind that each human Soul has 12 extensions/ parts, which together make up our Higher Self. Only one extension can occupy a physical body and up to 3 extensions can have different bodies/lifetimes on Earth at the same time. As each extension incarnates and grows to a higher spiritual level, the closer we become to reaching the God vibration. Lucifer was able to have physical lifetimes as a Light Being at the same time another part of his Soul was having a lifetime of darkness. This process of other parts of his soul having Light experiences helped to keep his soul in balance and not fall completely into darkness.

As an example, during the lifetime of Jesus, I think we

have all heard about Judas who betrayed Jesus and divulged Jesus' whereabouts to the Roman authorities which led to His crucifixion.

According to Jesus, Judas was a friend He could trust and He asked Judas to go and tell the Roman authorities where they could find him. Jesus knew that if He went into hiding the Romans would make life for His family and friends miserable, and He wanted to spare them from harassment, torture, and undue harm.

What history did not tell us was that once Judas realized that his actions resulted in the torture, humiliation, and death of Jesus, he was so distraught he committed suicide. It was his love, compassion, loyalty to Jesus that caused him to make the ultimate sacrifice of taking his own life. Instead, history labeled Judas as a betrayer – a negative label for sure. However, Jesus, being the loving Soul that He is, wanted to right the wrong that had been thrust upon Judas. He wanted to clear the negative energy which surrounded that incident and to let the TRUTH be known. Judas was one of the extensions of Lucifer's Soul.

FAILURE/SUCCESS OF LUCIFER

If the experience on Earth was a test to see if humanity would follow God and the path of Light, Lucifer fought a good fight, but ultimately lost. He lost not only the battle but the war of evil, if, in fact, there was a war. It is just part of the illusion we experience while in human form.

Lucifer failed in his personal mission on Earth just as

Hitler had. Darkness equals failure. However, he did succeed in proving that without our connection to God, life is filled with struggle, heartache, and suffering.

ASCENSION INTO THE LIGHT

Lucifer has now ascended into the Light. He had to go through the restoration of the Soul process, just as the rest of humanity is required to do before entering the Light, but he has recently been welcomed "home."

We need to always keep in mind that even those Souls who chose the role of darkness are part of the oneness of all and grow as a result of their efforts, just as those who are working toward Light also grow.

ENERGIES ASSOCIATED WITH LUCIFER

Throughout history many humans used the names of Satan and the Devil (as well as many others) interchangeably with Lucifer as if they were one and the same. Spirit wanted to clarify the difference between Lucifer, the God-created Light Being, from these other entities.

The entity known as Satan is NOT a soul created by God. It is a thought form created by humanity. Thought forms are real as they are created from energy. One of my favorite sayings is: "Your Thoughts Create Your Reality," as I have found this to be very true in my life.

Therefore, if thought forms are "real," the negative ones need to be cleared/transformed through the positive vibrations of Love, Light, Peace, Joy, Forgiveness, Compassion, etc. Because Satan was such a strong, negative thought form, referred to by much of humanity, it took on a very powerful life form of its own.

When the Beings of Darkness were given word that their reign on Earth was over and their leader was no longer operating on Earth, the energy of Satan accompanied other dark beings into the Light and requested to be transformed into a Soul of Light. His wish was granted.

The Devil, too, was not Soul energy created by God. It was an accumulation of fearful dark thought forms created by humanity. Such as cartoon characters are created with his red suit, long tail and famous pitchfork – a great Halloween costume.

To the best of my knowledge, the energy of the Devil has not put in a request to become a Soul of Light. Therefore, its energy will be dissolved, as all Souls who, through their Free Will, will be dissolved if they chose not to return to the Light. It is the responsibility of humanity to dissolve the thought forms created on Earth by transforming the thoughts from negative to positive. However, humanity does not have the authority to dissolve Soul energy which has been created by God. God will be responsible for dissolving Souls who wish to remain in Darkness. Hopefully, there will not be too many who make that choice.

A MESSAGE FROM SANANDA

Following is a message received from Jesus/Sananda regarding Lucifer's purpose:

Lucifer's purpose was not an evil one. His purpose was to be one opposite of the spectrum of Light and Dark.

Lucifer was a very high level Light Being. He was not jealous of me or anyone else. His mission was to fulfill a very important experience on Earth. Because of his higher vibration, we all felt this would be an easy mission for him. Unfortunately, playing the role of Darkness is not an easy thing to do.

Even though he had a non-Light position to experience on Earth, he and I as well as many of his Soul Group members, kept in touch on this side to review what was taking place on Earth. Because he was created as a Light Being, it was very difficult for him, in human form, to generate followers of the dark side.

Unfortunately, humanity found it very easy to get used to the negative side of life. Humans did not remember who they were while in residence in their spirit bodies. The heaviness of the human uniform made it difficult for them to follow the guidance that was so carefully chosen before their descent to Earth.

We are very pleased to see that things are finally beginning to work according to the Plan God/Creator originally envisioned for Planet Earth and humanity. Humanity, at this particular time, is not able to see the big picture of Heaven on Earth as many are still in struggle mode. They will release themselves from this vibration and they, too, will be able to KNOW who they are and their purpose for being on Earth.

In the meantime, we will continue to offer whatever support, Love and guidance that they are willing to accept.

Sananda

5/7/15

Chapter 3

DUALITY

The purpose of duality is a simple one – to have two opposite ends meet in the middle and this meeting ground is called "Balance."

When we look at something good and we can also see something bad, these two perspectives join and become one – this is referred to as balanced energy. The item/situation is neither good nor bad, it just is. When humanity reaches the level where we are able to see all opposites as neutral, then we will have attained true mastership. All is working for good, but it takes many lifetimes for individuals to realize this truth. It is so much easier to see things as good or bad, right or wrong, etc.

Even though two individuals may have two different opinions on the same subject, they are both right. This is very hard to comprehend as the normal train of thought is good or bad – right or wrong. There is no middle ground between the two ends of the spectrum.

However, when an individual reaches the middle of the spectrum, when they are able to understand that everyone will reach that middle ground in their own time and until then, whatever their opinion is, it is RIGHT for them. They will change their opinion, if necessary, when it is time for their awakening on that particular idea/subject.

Awakening is a slow process. It does not happen overnight or in a few days, weeks, months or even years. It happens one step at a time and when this process is complete, you are still not completed with the evolution plan God has set forth for humanity. There are many other steps along the path and they will be achieved for each and every human.

The path to spiritual evolution has been accelerated due to the many individuals who have already awakened and who are helping those around them to understand what they have found to be their TRUTH.

Each individual needs to weigh information they receive from others as to how it feels for them and how it fits in their belief system. If it seems right, take it in and add it to your beliefs. If not, then just let it go and do not judge simply because it may not feel right, that it is "wrong." Just let it go and be content with your beliefs. Again, there is no right or wrong, there just IS!

DUALITY A MAIN REASON FOR OUR INCARNATION

Duality is one of the main reasons why we incarnated on Planet Earth. Our purpose is to overcome duality – override the dark with the Light until we reach the state of balance. This is easier said than done. However, through our life experiences – learning our lessons and balancing our Karma – we are able to reach the level of enlightenment and that is when we are done with our lifetimes on Earth.

To break free of the experience of duality, it is important to follow the guidance of your heart, for that is where the Soul resides. The Soul knows the path to Ascension and if you allow it, the Soul will lead you to the Light.

Separation is an illusion. It is one of life's tricks to keep us stuck in the mentality of duality. Through the evolutionary process we reach the level of oneness.

When I was first introduced to the concept of oneness, I disagreed totally with my Guides. How could that be? I was a separate individual with my own energy, thoughts, beliefs, etc., and I was definitely not connected with anyone else except through relationships. My guidance allowed me to hang onto that belief, knowing that I would change my belief in my own time. As I grew spiritually, it became obvious that it is true – we are all ONE – ONE with God and One with each other!

BOTH LIGHT AND DARK QUALITIES

Every human carries aspects of both Light and dark

qualities. The Light aspects represent the positive qualities, such as: Love, Compassion, Hope, Joy, etc.; whereas, the dark aspects represent the negative qualities, such as: fear, anger, conflict, judgment, hatred, deceit/lies, etc.

If you are on Earth as a human, you have not yet blended the dark with the Light. Once you are able to do this (and many are achieving balance during this lifetime), you will be a full-fledged Ascended Master and will not have to return to Earth for future incarnations. What a glorious day that will be! However, you will have choices to make as to what your next steps will be. A few options are:

- You can stay on the Other Side and act as a Master Guide to those in your Soul Group who are still reincarnating on Earth.
- Up until you reach the top of the 6th level of vibration you will still be able to reincarnate on Earth, again to help your Soul Group members reach the level of Ascension.
- Or now that you are a multi-dimensional being you will be able to visit other Universes to advance your vibration to even higher levels.

THE FEAR VIBRATION

The ego part of us carries the fear vibration. It is not bad. It is the part/role the ego has for humanity. It is our responsibility through our thoughts, actions, words, and feelings to overcome the fears we are facing through Faith, Love, Compassion, Understanding, Forgiveness, etc. –

through the Light qualities.

This is easier said than done, as the ego part of us has been in charge for all of our many existences on Earth. However, NOW is the time to override the feelings created by ego and reach up and connect with our Higher (God) Self and create our new reality filled with positive Light qualities. This will happen naturally through the Ascension Process, however, you can help it along by making a conscious effort (an intention) to create your reality through the Forces of Light!

Not always, but many times, when we engage in conflict with others, it is the ego's need to be in control. To overcome duality, remember that there is no right or wrong. That is part of the illusion we are dealing with here on Earth. Everything just IS!

Every human has the right to experience situations that are in their highest good. You may experience them differently, but it does not make your way better or right compared to what others are experiencing. Finding the lesson buried within the uncomfortable situation is the answer to overcoming it and moving forward along your spiritual path.

LAW OF DUALITY

The Law of Duality is about reaching a point of balance, not choosing one of the extremes. It's about finding the center.

Light is the absence of darkness and darkness is the

absence of Light.

Wisdom is the absence of ignorance and ignorance is the absence of Wisdom.

Two things which "appear" to be opposites are only two extremes of the same thing. Some examples of opposites:

Happy/Sad

Black/White

Large/Small

High/Low

Dry/Wet

Victim/Villain

Positive/Negative

Calm/Chaos

Justice/Punishment

Hot/Cold

Life/Death

Day/Night

Short/Tall

Male/Female

Near/Far

Right/Wrong

Good/Bad

Beautiful/Ugly

Light/Dark

Love/Hate

For/Against

Clarity/Confusion
Prosperity/Poverty
Winner/Loser
Above/Below
Peace/War
Better/Worse
Left/Right
More/Less
Ignorance/Wisdom
Etc., Etc., Etc.

During our life experiences, it is our (humanity's) responsibility to balance the effect of duality – not eliminate it. Example: Light cannot eliminate darkness. When we walk into a dark room and turn the light switch on the darkness disappears. However, as soon as we turn the light switch off, the darkness in the room reappears. Also we cannot eliminate the darkness of night. We have to wait for the morning sun to come up. Therefore, we are to bring balance to the darkness by using Light when necessary and allowing darkness to exist naturally.

Once we transcend our struggle with duality, we enter a state of peaceful unity. Again, it is important to keep in mind that there is no right or wrong to any situation – it just "IS." Whatever we are experiencing is exactly what we are supposed to be experiencing at any given time. The important thing is to find the lesson in the experience that we need to learn.

Duality – pairs of opposites which are identical in nature, but different in degree. Balance is when the two opposite extremes meet at the center point. This is when we have transcended duality.

Duality is an opportunity for humanity to grow to higher spiritual levels.

Duality manipulates and enslaves us until we learn to transcend it.

Duality serves as a teacher.

Duality serves the separation aspect of our human experience.

Duality creates conflict. By overcoming duality we can create Heaven on Earth.

Duality is a tool which helps us to achieve balance in life.

Duality is opposites of the same spectrum – Light/Dark.

Duality created the need for Free Will.

Duality helps us to reach our ultimate Soul purpose of Ascension. In order to reach the level of Ascension, we need to learn our life lessons, balance our karma, transcend the illusion of separation, and overcome the need for duality. When we reach this state of Ascension, we no longer need to return to Earth as we have succeeded in our mission.

Duality is used to manipulate our thoughts and beliefs; to control our emotions; to keep us under the umbrella of illusion; to keep us divided and in conflict with not only others, but ourselves as well.

The process of transcending duality is to change our thoughts and beliefs from negative to positive (from dark to Light).

Reincarnation is the Soul's decision to return time and time again in order to overcome duality.

Everything is dual. Everything has its pair of opposites – opposites that are identical in nature, but different in degree. We can transform the extremes of duality by consciously raising our vibration through our thoughts, words, actions, and feelings.

Duality may appear to be very real, but it is part of the illusion which is part of our earthly physical and mental experience.

From duality we transcend into unity and our job on Earth is done.

Duality does not exist in the Spirit World as All is One!

We experience the Law of Duality on a daily basis as we go through life, as it is part of the challenge humanity has to go through in order to reach our ultimate goal of Ascension and returning from separation to Oneness.

Have you ever had an experience where, at the time it was happening, it "appeared" to be the worst possible situation? As time progressed, you realized that it was the best possible thing that has ever happened. There is the balance. You have seen one situation from both ends of the spectrum.

An example I personally experienced was when it was time for my husband and me to divorce. It appeared to be the end of my world. I fell into a temporary three month state of depression. I was in a dark place and it didn't feel good at all. However, as time progressed and the darkness lifted, my life now is better than it ever has been. I love to travel and I have been able to do a lot of travelling and visit places that were once only a possible dream. I have written two books (this is my third and I have a fourth one on the back burner) and have become an award-winning author. I have experienced freedom to do whatever I want, whenever I want to. There were more positives that resulted from the divorce than there were negatives. One of the best outcomes is that my ex and I have become very good friends and have a mutual respect for one another that we didn't share during the marriage while going through our life lessons.

Review the situations in your life to see if any of them that appeared to be wrong or negative have turned into a positive outcome. Remember to make this review a habit!

PART II

DARKNESS

Chapter 4

DARKNESS

The subject of darkness is quite extensive as well as interesting for humanity. There are many different interpretations of darkness, including:

- Darkness is simply the absence of Light.
- Darkness is Evil. Evil is the absence of God. According to Albert Einstein, evil is the result of what happens when man does not have God's Love present in his heart. John 3:19 - "men loved darkness rather than Light, because their deeds were evil."
- Darkness is separate, outside of the human, sent to them by God as a form of punishment.
- Darkness is an individual opposite from God. God is GOOD, therefore, an individual of darkness is

BAD.

- Darkness is an individual with a name such as Lucifer, Satan, Devil, etc.
- Darkness is something that happens to "bad" people for not following God's laws.
- Darkness is something to be feared. DON'T be afraid of darkness. Embrace it and shine your Light on it. Darkness cannot exist when Light is present.
- Darkness is something we cannot control. If we deserve to have a negative experience in life, it will automatically happen to us. This is only half right. The truth is, if we have placed a Life Lesson in our Soul Contract which calls for a negative experience, we are in control. It is how we react to the circumstances placed before us which determine whether we lean toward the Light or toward darkness.
- Darkness is a symbol of the color black. This is not true as black is actually a very protective color. Hollywood may have had something to do with this myth. I remember watching cowboy movies with my father when I was young. The good guy always wore a white hat and rode a white horse. The villain in the movie always wore a black hat and rode a black horse. Even as a kid it was easy to figure that out.
- Darkness is part of the illusion we are experiencing

during our journey on Earth. Darkness/Duality does not exist in the Heavenly Realm. It is an experiment for humans while on Earth using the gift of Free Will to determine which path we want to follow.

- Darkness is a tool available to humanity for the purpose of learning, growing, and evolving to higher levels of spiritual awareness/consciousness.
- Darkness is the ego part of us. Ego carries the fight or flight trigger when we encounter conflict. Usually the ego part of us would rather "fight" than run. While our ego many times guides us in the direction of negative/dark thoughts and reactions, it is only following its purpose until such time as it melds with our Soul energy.

You may have your own interpretation of what darkness means to you according to what you have experienced in life. The meaning or interpretation of darkness is not as important as dissolving/transforming anything that "feels" uncomfortable from your daily experiences by bringing in the Light and Love of God to replace what "appears" to be darkness.

Chapter 5

DARKNESS – WHERE DOES IT COME FROM?

There are four major areas where we draw upon the energy of darkness:

1. **Within** – we can create darkness through our thoughts, actions, words, and feelings if they are not of a positive nature. The darkness we carry within, if not released through forgiveness or other positive emotions, attaches to the Soul and we carry it to the Other Side upon physical death, which hampers our spiritual growth and reason for being in human form.

2. **Above** – when we place experiences of darkness in our Life Plan, our Higher Self will trigger events to occur in order for us to have that experience and to (hopefully) grow to a higher spiritual vibration

as a result of having gone through the negative experience.

3. **Others around us** – through the people we interact with on a daily basis. Remember we have Soul Contracts with others for the purpose of learning lessons, balancing Karma, and growing to higher spiritual levels while on Earth.

  In addition to those individuals in our life, we have others who are operating under the umbrella of darkness who make the rules and laws that we have to live by. These are the most difficult individuals as they do not have our highest best interests in mind. They are only concerned with their highest and wealthiest best interests and the ability to remain in control.

4. **Fear** – Humanity created the vibration of fear. It is a vibration we slip into whenever we encounter individuals or experiences that are uncomfortable or traumatic even if these events are only perceived as a real threat. As we release and let go of our fears, we are able to rise to higher spiritual vibrations.

While writing the book *Soul Releasement: Assisting Souls into the Light*, I had indicated that I did not believe in demonic/evil souls. I'm not saying they don't exist, I'm saying that I had not had any experiences with evil souls. Some may have appeared evil, but these souls were frustrated. After counseling, they understood that they needed to go to the Light and not stay earthbound.

Shortly after writing the statement that I did not believe in demonic/evil souls, I received an email from a person in South America asking for my help in releasing some demonic souls from their energy field. This person had gone to several other practitioners who were not able to help. I am not a "hero." If several others were not able to release these entities, I didn't know what I could do.

In checking with the Higher Self of the individual, I was told there were no attachments. What this individual was experiencing was included in their Life Plan, which had been activated.

Instead of resisting the darkness, we need to embrace it. Thank it for coming forward to teach us what we don't want and let it go. By asking the Higher Self for help in releasing the dark experience, the Higher Self will make sure you have learned what you need to before letting it go completely.

Many times earthbound entities can cause us pain and suffering which may appear as darkness, the Devil/Satan at work. However, it is just lost Souls afraid of what awaits them on the Other Side. They stay earthbound and when they realize they can continue life without a physical body by attaching to another human, they do not realize this is bad, wrong or evil. However, many times this action causes the host much discomfort.

Many individuals who allow darkness to work through

them are very good people and have what they consider the best intentions. They get caught up in the stresses which confront them on a daily basis. If the stress is not released, the individual may react in a very negative, violent way.

We are not only ascending into the Light, we are (at the same time) ascending out of darkness.

Jesus/Sananda had told me that changes in the destiny of humanity can be requested from Source by the Beings of Light overseeing the evolution of Souls on Earth. One change which was necessary was the requirements for Ascension, which were revised from individual Soul Ascension to Mass or Group Ascension (1950). The requirements expected from Souls were cut almost in half.

Another decision made by the higher Beings of Light was that humanity, in physical form, was not able to overcome the Dark Forces which prevailed on Earth without the assistance of our Heavenly Helpers. The Beings of Light had to play a stronger role in helping humanity overcome the darkness. Therefore, with anything that would harm the entire Planet or the majority of humanity, our Heavenly Helpers are able to step in and give us a helping hand without our asking. With smaller events which would involve only sections of Earth or a number of humans (not the majority), we would have to take care of on our own, BUT with the assistance of the Heavenly Helpers should we call upon them.

Incarnating Souls carry contracts to work with the

Beings of Light in order to expose those manipulating the system and keeping the majority of humanity in poverty and/or poor health. They are referred to as "whistle blowers." Hopefully, we will be hearing from more of them in the future.

There are high-level Light Beings who will also overshadow some of our world leaders in order to assist in exposing the darkness which has operated on Earth far too long. The Great Experiment has ended and it is time for darkness on Earth to be dissolved. Let us do our part in bringing a higher vibration of Light to the Planet.

Multi-millions of years ago, it was decided that Earth would be a Planet to house humans of both Light and Dark Forces. The Dark Forces would have free reign to conduct business as they wished, but there would be a time frame associated with their activities.

The gift of Free Will was given to all of humanity in order for all humans to make decisions that would suit their own needs. The Plan was for the Forces of Dark to eventually join with the Forces of Light to create an even stronger band of Light on Planet Earth. We are at the time now when the Dark Forces need to combine with the Light Forces or be dissolved.

The energy of darkness became so powerful on Earth that it took many lifetimes of individuals reincarnating before they could reach the level of Light. Two different times in Earth's history (Lemuria & Atlantis) humanity had reached high vibrational levels, but unfortunately both eras were dramatically affected by those operating under the umbrella of darkness, which almost caused humanity to become extinct. After the fall of Atlantis, humanity sank from the Fifth Dimension back to the Third Dimension. It is as if we had to start our growth process all over again.

Through our Life Plan we experience life lessons which we included for that particular lifetime. Since it was not possible to learn everything we needed to learn in one lifetime, reincarnation was added to our Plans. We could return to Earth as many times as possible until we learned everything that needed to be learned – both good/positive and bad/negative experiences. The expectation was that, if we had a negative experience it would not feel comfortable, we would learn from the experience and move forward in a more positive direction.

Unfortunately, the negative in all areas of life became the norm; to the point where many have lost their way. It appeared that we handed our power over to the government officials that we elected to look out for us and protect us from harm. We believed that because these individuals were well-educated, well-spoken, many times from the wealthy echelon, we thought they knew more than we did and gave them complete power over our life. Over the years it only got worse to the point that today we are afraid of what the government will do if we don't follow the rules and laws that they make for "our own good."

As sad as that is, unfortunately it has become our reality in the United States. Organizations such as the Internal Revenue Service, Federal Bureau of Investigation, Central Intelligence Agency, etc., etc., have created an atmosphere of fear and distrust by those who are supposed to be "serving" us. While the elected government officials often take the blame for what is not right during their administration, it is the Illuminati, the Dark Cabal, the Shadow Government (whatever you want to call it) who are really the ones in CHARGE!

Humanity has the ability to "grow" out of the clutches of darkness as we follow the path of Ascension and raise our Light quotient and vibration. As we add Light to our physical bodies, it helps Mother Earth to raise her vibration as well.

We need to fill our heart with the Love and Light of God and then shine that Light across the entire Planet, directing it to all of God's creations, including the Dark Forces. An exercise I do daily is: I open the door to my heart. Invite the Light and Love of God to come in to overflowing capacity. I take what I need for my own benefit. Then the overflow is directed to anyone I have face-to-face, thought, or electronic communication with. Finally the balance of the overflow is spread across the Planet to all of God's creations, including the darkness.

FEAR – FALSE EVIDENCE APPEARING REAL

Fear is the fuel needed by the Dark Forces. It is their greatest weapon against us. They get high on the fear we generate as a result of their actions. Therefore, it is extremely important that we do everything in our power not to react in a fearful manner.

Worry is a milder form of fear, but nonetheless, it is still classified as a form of "fear." So worrying about the challenges or people in your life is not doing any good at all. As humans we think that worrying is a form of Love. It means that we care about those who we are worrying about.

Instead of worrying about our loved ones, thinking something "bad" might happen to them when they are not with us, it would be better to ask their Angels to watch over them and keep them safe; then KNOW and TRUST that they will be. Remember: what we think about, focus on, and put our energy into becomes our reality. So think positive!

Illness is a form of "darkness" destined to lead us to Light. Illness usually creates fear within us. Fear that our condition may be worse than we think it is. Fear that our condition may cause our death. Fear that, if we overcome/ get better, that the illness will return at some point in the future.

The secret to overcoming the fear vibration is to mentally reach up to the higher realms of Light and ask that God's Love and Light vibration shine on you and massage the painful area of your body with the intention that God's Love and Light vibration will heal you.

Love will dissolve the darkness – the fear vibration. So

if you are experiencing any type of illness, let go of the fear of that condition and reach upward to the Light, to God, and replace the fear vibration with that of faith – faith that God loves you and wants the very best for you, and if it is at all possible for you to be healed, you will be. It could be a healing as included in your Soul Contract, or you could be granted an extension of life, known as a "miraculous" healing.

Illness is a form of spiritual awakening if we allow it to be by placing our self (our condition) in God's hands for healing. If it is not part of our Soul Plan to be healed, then our illness is what we have chosen as our exit back to the higher dimensions. However, our transition will be much easier as a result of our connection with our God Self.

FEAR is a weapon used to keep us in line. The media is the instrument used to project this fear. The nightly national news usually is all about the negative things happening in the world. Whether these events actually happened or not is not the issue. It is what the powers-that-be want us to believe and to be fearful of so that they can come forward and be our heroes in a way that will serve an agenda not necessarily ours (the people).

At this time darkness controls the world and humanity. It is up to us to stamp out the darkness which has ruled Planet Earth for so long, not with warfare or fighting, but with Compassion, Forgiveness, Understanding, Kindness, Love, and Light.

Humans have many fears. We seem to worry about anything and everything, even things that have not happened or things that "might" happen. However, those at the top of the darkness project are very confident and appear to be fearless. They operate above, outside of, and beyond the laws that they created for us to abide by so they don't have to worry about any consequences regarding their illegal actions.

However, they do have one FEAR and that is we (humanity) will wake up to how they have controlled and manipulated us for most of our existence as humans and they will lose not only their power but control over us. It is time for us to REBEL and bring them down in the most graceful way.

Very important is the fact that the dark Secret Societies control our level of fear through the media, movies, and the outcome of what happens when we don't follow the rules they enforce for our own protection. We can take control out of their hands by eliminating the fears that they present to us. We can't believe everything we are told by our officials.

My Master Guide, Jonathan, gave me the following message regarding fear while I was in meditation in Sedona, Arizona on May 4, 2015:

Know that there are many Light Beings who have asked that they have an opportunity to state their feelings about letting go of fear which is what creates darkness. Once humans relax and let go of their fears of everything, then darkness will no longer have a purpose on Earth and that is what will Create Heaven on Earth.

Jesus had told me that it was the power of fear that allowed Hitler and his army to terrorize and kill multi-millions of people. With the situation we are experiencing now, we have only hundreds of individuals controlling 7.5 billion people. Once again, the fear factor is in play. The powerful sources of Light are willing to support us. If we join forces with them, we can be assured of a positive outcome.

While in Sedona, Arizona with a friend, we visited several of the energy vortexes. Following is a message I received from Sananda regarding the subject of "Fear."

There is absolutely nothing to fear where darkness is concerned. Humans created fear regarding anything that they didn't understand or that hurt in one way or another – physically, mentally, emotionally, or spiritually.

Since humans created fear regarding anything that was uncomfortable, then humans have that same ability to dissolve that which they have created. This is what is possible on this side of the veil – to be able to create something and then dissolve it whether it is for practice or whether due to a mistake.

This is part of the experience of Creating Heaven on Earth – a part of the experience of becoming a God. Once humans have mastered the ability to undo what they have created on Earth, they will be ready to start creating planets, galaxies, universes on this side of the veil. The veil, as it is called, was a barrier between Heaven and Hell (Earth). Humanity will be responsible for breaking this barrier and allowing Heaven and Earth to be ONE!

Jesus/Sananda

Chapter 6

DARK NIGHT OF THE SOUL

The phrase "Dark Night of the Soul" was originated by a 16th century Spanish mystic named John of the Cross, also called St. John of the Cross. Unfortunately, all humans have to go through this type of experience at some point during their many lifetimes.

The Dark Night of the Soul is an empty, lonely feeling as if you have lost your connection with God, your Higher Self, your Angels and Spirit Guides. In the past, when you have called out to them for help, they have always responded to your every request. But now they do not answer. It "appears" as if they have all abandoned you.

In reality, they have NOT abandoned you. They are there and assisting you, but not through two-way communication. Keep your faith and KNOW that you are not alone no matter how things "appear" to be. You are loved, you are protected and you are guided.

Everyone, at some time or another in their life, goes through the experience of the "Dark Night of the Soul."

One of the first written examples of this was the Bible story of Job. Job was a very blessed, God-loving, and righteous man. He had a wonderful family, good health, and wealth in the form of livestock and property. Life was good. However, as a life experience/lesson/test of faith, he lost everything except his life.

In spite of his dire circumstances, Job did not curse God, but instead cursed the day he was born. For some reason Job felt that what he was experiencing was God's Will and accepted his fate. Long story short, because of Job's faithfulness to God, his circumstances were restored to better than he originally had.

Many individuals are and have been experiencing the Dark Night of the Soul through loss of their jobs, homes and/or the loss of loved ones. Keep the faith and keep reaching up and asking for whatever you need. There is a time-frame associated with the so-called Dark Night of the Soul. The more positive we are, the less we have to endure. The more negative we are, the more prolonged the circumstances are.

Remember the circumstances we are going through are not a punishment from God, but something we have chosen to experience for the purpose of spiritual growth. We agreed to these circumstances before we were born.

I know it is extremely difficult to be grateful for the loss of anything, especially a loved one. However, it is possible to be grateful for the time we had with them, the love we shared, and the memories we created together. By embracing the experience with Light, no matter how upsetting it may be, will get us through this "Dark Night" in a more positive way.

I would like to share an example with you. A long-time friend of mine lost her grandson, at age 19, due to a drowning. This shocked anyone who knew him as he was quite the athlete and had played sports since he was three years old.

The autopsy showed that his passing was Sudden Cardiac Arrest due to undetected Hypertrophic Cardiomyopathy. Sudden Cardiac Arrest takes the life of a young person every three days. In most cases, the heart condition goes undetected unless testing beyond a physical exam is conducted.

His family established a non-profit foundation in his memory in hopes of saving other children from Sudden Cardiac Arrest.

Through their fund-raising efforts, the family is able to conduct free heart screenings for young adults 13-19 years old, to teach CPR, and to purchase and donate AEDs (Automated External Defibrillators) to schools and non-profit organizations.

In December 2014, the mother was honored by the Boston Celtics Basketball team with their *"Heroes Among Us"* award for volunteerism. In June 2015, she received the top honor from the "New England Patriots Myra Kraft Community MVP Award" for her volunteer work.

Her mission continues as she is working on getting legislation passed that would require coaches to be trained in CPR and to require CPR training in high schools.

She was able to turn her Dark Night into a Bright Day for others to benefit.

The "Dark Night" is a growth experience for the Soul. After having had the Love and protection of God, you feel as though you have been abandoned. What did or will you do? Keep the faith. Know that you have definitely not been abandoned. You are only without power for a short period of time. It is like, here on Earth, when we lose our electrical power due to a storm or downed lines, we continue with whatever we can do and wait for the "lights"/power to come back on. God will restore your lines of communication as soon as the Soul has benefited from the experience.

In Isaiah 45:3 (King James Version), God says "I will give you the treasures of darkness." So when you are experiencing your Dark Night of the Soul, remember that it will turn out to be one of the treasures life has to offer as it will bring you to enlightenment, and that is humanity's purpose – enlightenment!

The dark times of life are an opportunity to grow to

higher spiritual levels depending upon how we react to them. Resisting them only makes things worse and brings us more darkness. Our embracing darkness with Light and Love will assist in dissolving the darkness much sooner.

The phrase "Dark Night of the Soul" is often confusing as it definitely lasts longer than one night or day for that matter. It lasts as long as we resist darkness by fearing it, pushing it away, or pretending that it does not exist. When we embrace it, recognize it, and dismiss it, we are free and are able to move forward on our spiritual path and do what we are destined to do while here on Earth.

Chapter 7

HOW CAN WE OVERCOME DARKNESS?

Once humanity learns that Light and Love are two very powerful secret weapons to solving all of our problems, which stem from darkness, there will be no need for darkness to exist on Earth any longer. The lessons will have been learned and there will be no further need to journey to Earth.

Some of the things humans can do to "fight" the darkness:

1. Keep our thoughts as positive and clean as possible.
2. Pray for anyone you know or have contact with who seems to be operating under the umbrella of

darkness.

3. Set up a prayer group in your community if one is not already established. Prayer is not just meant to take place in church. Prayers can be expressed anywhere at any time. So please make this a habit in your daily routine.

4. Connect with the Spiritual Light Beings assigned to you and ask for protection for yourself and your loved ones.

5. Do whatever you possibly can for others who are in need of help. Just being a good friend/listener can help them unburden themselves of their struggles. Sometimes just being able to talk to someone is a major help.

6. Release and let go of your problems as soon as possible. Holding onto them and re-living them over and over in your mind is not healthy. When you are ready, release them through the breath. Deep breathing is an excellent way to clear negativity and prevent it from taking up permanent residence within us.

   Simple Breathing Exercise: Focus your attention on anything of a negative nature that is bothering you. Take in a very deep breath. Then attach your intention of letting go of your negative thoughts/experiences as you exhale, forcefully. Repeat several times until you feel "lighter."

7. Pray for World Peace.

8. Be kind to your fellow man. Kindness is contagious; just as a smile and yawn will cause others around you to do the same, even if they don't know what they are smiling about and even if they are not tired. It will not only make you feel good, but the recipient of your kindness will also benefit.

9. Each community should set up a special fund (through fundraising events) to help anyone in that community who needs a helping hand, whether it be a temporary helping hand or something more permanent. This will only be necessary on a temporary basis until such time as the Illuminati/Dark Cabal is out of business and things are being run as they should be – "for the people and by the people."

10. Most important – TAKE ACTION! If we are aware of a situation that is inappropriate, it is important that we speak up and form a support group to voice our opinion whatever the situation is. We have been taken advantage of long enough. Once we start speaking up, we will have the power to change circumstances for all in a positive way.

ADDITIONAL THINGS WE CAN DO TO STAMP OUT DARKNESS

We can each do many things to balance out the negative with positive thoughts, actions, words, and feelings. All of these actions are energy which will equate to positive circumstances happening not only in our life, but those around us as well. Always keep in mind that Light is positive, the Dark is negative, and the way to balance the darkness is through Light.

This seems very simple and, once we make it part of our daily routine, it is. However, it has been so long since humanity has been able to see the positive in their daily lives that they think it is impossible. It is definitely NOT impossible. It is only impossible IF you "think" it is and don't make any effort to change things.

Below I have listed several suggestions of things we can do to "Stamp Out Darkness:"

LOVE & LIGHT

LOVE is one of the weapons to be used to "fight" darkness and the Dark Forces. It seems as though we, as individuals, don't have the power to fight darkness fully. However, as we join forces with our Heavenly Helpers, we will rise above the darkness, and Peace shall exist on Earth.

It is important to know that we cannot expect the Heavenly Helpers to do this for us. We have to do our part as well. That is one of the main reasons we have chosen this mission of Creating Heaven on Earth. However, as we take whatever actions we can, then our Heavenly Helpers will be able to step in and help us even more.

We who follow the path of Light can band together in prayer and hold a vision of Heaven on Earth. The energies of Light and Love are two of the most powerful weapons of choice against darkness. They are more powerful than any military weapons created for the purpose of mass killing and destruction.

It is not a time for hate, revenge, resentment or any other negative emotion. It is a time to show the Dark Ones that Love & Light are more powerful than they will ever be. Now that we are aware of how they were able to control and manipulate us, it is time to show them that we choose to take our power back.

FORGIVENESS

Forgiving the individuals who have been operating under the umbrella of darkness will ensure that we maintain our vibrational level of energy. To get angry, resentful, or revengeful towards these individuals of darkness would only bring our energy down to a lower vibration and that would not be in our highest best interest, but it would serve the interests of the Dark Cabal.

COMPASSION & UNDERSTANDING

Know that the individuals operating in the energy of darkness need compassion and understanding from us. To sit in judgment and criticize their actions will serve no benefit to anyone. Don't challenge them as darkness thrives on conflict. Allow them to be as they want to be, but DO NOT let them drag you down to their level. Quietly send them God's Love and Light and let them be.

PEACE

As you walk, put each foot forward in the vibration that PEACE is your birthright and that as long as you move in a forward direction – PEACE will be yours!

In meditation, spread a Blanket of Peace all around you. Then ask the Angels and Archangels to take this Blanket of Peace and spread it across the entire planet. By spreading Peace around the world – PEACE shall reign. You may not think you can do much as an individual, but this is a unity effort. It is what is going to bring all the individual parts of humanity together to unite as ONE!

POSITIVE THINKING

Since our thoughts create our reality, think as POSITIVE as you possibly can with regard to any/all situations that are placed before you. Know that your positive thoughts will spread and have an effect on those around you for the good of all.

ALIGN YOUR ENERGY WITH YOUR GOD SELF

The stronger our connection with God, the more powerful we become. Develop a strong connection, not only with your own Higher (God) Self, but with the Creator God who oversees the Universe that Earth is connected to. The stronger our Soul link to the God/Source, the stronger our manifesting abilities will be.

We are able to create the type of life we want. Having the finer things in life is possible for all; however, it is our responsibility to obtain our wishes, goals, through Light methods, not through the means of darkness. In other words, if we work and earn money to purchase more than the necessities of life, OR if we don't have the money to purchase what we want, we can put our desires out to the Universe for manifestation, – these are Light methods.

However, if we get involved in illegal activities in order to have the money needed for the luxury items we desire, this is using dark methods.

Another benefit of aligning with our Higher (God) Self is Peace of Mind (inner peace). I remember as my Soul was guided to step onto its spiritual path, I had a very hard time at work (in the corporate world). One night I had a meltdown and reached up and asked God for inner peace, not knowing that inner peace was a positive side effect to the challenges I had been experiencing. Pain and suffering are part of humanity's process for spiritual growth. As long as we are in physical bodies on Earth, we will be faced with challenges. However, the higher our vibration, the less pain and suffering we experience.

EMBRACE THE DARKNESS

Let go of that which does not serve your higher good. This will release the hold of darkness on you. Through the collective consciousness of humanity, it is the responsibility of every human to do their best in overcoming duality.

DON'T be afraid of the "darkness." Embrace it and shine your Light on it. Darkness cannot exist when Light is present.

WILL DARKNESS FOLLOW US ALONG OUR SPIRITUAL PATH?

Only until such time as we have gone through the Ascension Process. Part of the Ascension Process is for the Ego to work in tandem with the Soul and then for the Soul/Ego to join with the Higher Self and allow the Higher Self to lead the journey on Earth. This integration of energies leads us to higher spiritual levels and balances the Dark with Light. Once we are in balance, the experiences we once thought of as dark will have little or no effect on us.

Darkness can befall individuals of all walks of life – even those who have a strong connection with God and the Heavenly Helpers. As humans, we have to experience the "bad" along with the "good" in order to make our Free Will choices of which path we want to follow.

PART III

SECRET SOCIETIES

Chapter 8

SECRET SOCIETIES

While a number of Secret Societies exist throughout the world, here are three of the most important ones that work through the Shadow Government to control all major events on Earth.

Illuminati

Committee of 300

The Bilderberg Group

They control all major media. The news we see on TV, hear on the radio, or read in the newspapers is what they want us to know and not necessarily the TRUTH! Sometimes events are deliberately created in order to divert our attention from what is REALLY happening. In addition, these three societies control just about every aspect of life on Earth, including our governments.

Some others are mystery groups like Skull & Bones,

a Yale University Society established in 1832. Many Skull & Bones secret members move into positions of power, such as President and government inner circles such as the cabinet.

Freemasons, established in 1717, was a legitimate upstanding private society until it was infiltrated by the Illuminati/Dark Cabal. For the majority of members it is still a legitimate upstanding organization. Only a few at the top are aware of the dark activities under the Freemasons' umbrella.

There are too many Secret Societies in different countries to list. However, these three groups (Illuminati, Committee of 300, and The Bilderberg Group), along with the help of the Dark Reptilians, control Planet Earth. They have many self-serving goals, but the main one is to establish a One World Government, which would give them complete control over the Planet.

The history of darkness on Earth, and the necessity for so many Secret Societies, is the result of a plan to amass the majority of wealth/resources by a few elite and privileged individuals focused on controlling the entire population on Earth.

Many of the individuals who hold office in our governments are not looking out for the welfare of U.S. citizens, but the welfare of the large corporations and banks and making sure they follow the wishes of the Illuminati, those few who dictate their desires and demands to everyone else.

FEDERAL RESERVE BANK & THE TITANIC

The Federal Reserve Bank was founded in 1910 in a secret meeting with some of the wealthiest individuals in the world. It is a privately owned bank, NOT a U.S. Federal Bank.

A major event with regard to the Federal Reserve Bank Act being passed has to do with the sinking of the Titanic on April 12, 1912.

The Titanic sank due to a collision with an iceberg. Some of the members who were AGAINST the creation of the Federal Reserve Banking system were on the ship for the purpose of meeting to discuss the passing of the U.S. Federal Reserve Bank Act. It is highly speculated that the sinking of the Titanic was a plot to ensure those members who opposed the idea of the Federal Reserve Bank would not survive to cast their vote accordingly.

It seems absolutely ludicrous that so many people had to die so that the ones who demanded the establishment of the Federal Reserve Bank could get the Federal Reserve Act passed.

Following is a message received from Sananda regarding the sinking of the Titanic:

Barbara, this is Sananda. Let's talk about the Titanic. That tragedy was unnecessarily caused by the Illuminati. It was a way of getting their way. No regard for human life. It was a plan to turn the tables in the direction which would serve their purposes. This is a story that few know of. However, nothing – absolutely nothing – is a secret forever. It is time for this story to be told.

Many of the individuals involved are no longer on Earth, but it will not do their reputations any good for they were seen as heroes, not only by their peers, but by much of humanity as well. We will not include names of individuals for they would not be eligible for prosecution anyway. So we will just tell the story as it happened.

It all has to do with control by the Illuminati. The Federal Reserve Bank is a storehouse for money being paid to the Illuminati for their needs. They are keeping this money hidden from the public (not just the American people) for the Federal Reserve Bank encompasses more than just the United States.

The people of the U.S. believe it is a bank to hold reserves of money for their protection, but this is NOT true. When things begin to collapse, this money would not be available for protection purposes.

As you know, we (on this side of the veil) are working diligently to right the wrong that has existed for so long. However, we are now in a position where we need humanity to not only wake up, but speak up as well. You may think that speaking up as an individual will only get you into trouble, but by speaking up as a group will bring success.

Prayer will also allow us to do even more to help humanity. In the not too distant future, you will witness the falling apart of the Illuminati/Dark Cabal and will see justice prevail. God had given darkness an opportunity to be part of the Free Will decision process, but this part of the Great Experiment could not go on indefinitely. That time is now up, but with so much darkness still residing on Earth, it will take a little longer than anticipated to create Heaven on Earth.

We are very excited as we are able to see the finale of the Great Experiment. We are able to see the oneness that is meant to be. We are able to see all Souls coming together for the good of all and this was the original plan and this is so!

Sananda

5/19/15

President Woodrow Wilson passed the Federal Reserve Act in 1913 which allowed the Federal Reserve Bank, a private banking cartel, to take over control of the nation's currency from the Federal Government. It was decided not to let the American citizens know that it was a private banking system. It would be better if we thought of it as a Federal Government Agency. The U.S. government has to borrow money (and pay interest) from this private banking institution to be able to continue running the country. It is our tax dollars which are funding this private institution.

FEDERAL INCOME TAX

Something else President Woodrow Wilson enacted during his presidency was the Income Tax Law. In all fairness to President Wilson, he was not aware of the hidden agenda at the time he implemented the Income Tax Law.

The ultimate "secret" purpose of this law was to keep the populace in poverty and to put the wealth into the hands of the Shadow Government. Prior to this law being passed, the money received from tariffs on trade goods was enough to run the country. The income tax was not part of the original plan for the citizens of the U.S.

While I am not opposed to paying federal or state income taxes, or any other taxes for that matter, for the purpose of running the country and providing the services necessary, I am opposed to our taxes being used to provide money for the members of the Shadow Government and Dark Cabal to take over control of the world. Their belief is that those who hold the wealth of the world will have control of the world. This is NOT acceptable so we (all of humanity) need to do our part in taking back control and making those in elected positions responsible for their actions instead of turning our heads the other way as if we don't know what's going on. Time to WAKE UP!

OTHER METHODS TO CONTROL THE WORLD

In an attempt to establish a New World Order by controlling resources including food, energy, water, health-care, large corporations, especially the financial systems, education, etc., the wealthy Dark Cabal literally used every method to bring down those who tried to take back their power/control. Some of the methods used are to discredit individuals, induce fatal diseases, heart attacks, create accidents/suicides, and the ultimate loss of life, including the assassination of President John F. Kennedy, John F. Kennedy Jr., Robert F. Kennedy, and Martin Luther King Jr., to name only a few.

The leaders of this world called Earth pretend to be working for our highest best interest and talk a good talk in convincing the public they are working hard on our behalf when, in fact, the opposite is the truth! They are looking out for their own personal gain.

Another important fact to keep in mind is that the majority, if not all, of our U.S. presidents are members of at least one of these secret societies. When they take their oath as President they swear to uphold the U.S. Constitution. But how can they, if they are obligated to, first and foremost, uphold their oath to the secret societies they belong to – most of which are working toward the One World Government? There is definitely a conflict of interest here.

Even though President Obama may not always have been popular, he has made attempts to bring control back to the elected officials and out of the hands of the Shadow Government. However, his attempts have been blocked by the Dark Cabal.

Obamacare was originally a good plan, designed for all Americans to have access to healthcare. When it was realized that control would be taken away from the insurance companies, steps were taken to change the plan.

Once again, the burden is NOT placed on the pharmaceutical companies, hospitals, and doctors to take a cut in their fees, it is put upon the working individuals to pay more so that all can be insured. This has angered many of the working class and rightfully so.

President Obama is a reincarnation of Abraham Lincoln's Soul energy, as was President John F. Kennedy. Jesus/Sananda has indicated to me many times that President Obama's mission was to begin the process of getting us back to what the original forefathers intended for the United States of America – "For the People, By the People." Unfortunately, he has been blocked from accomplishing his mission by those who are really in "control."

Once control was taken from the people, it appears to be a hard road in getting back on track. While our wonderful allies – the Light Beings in Spirit form – are helping all that they can, it truly is our (humanity's) responsibility to take the control and lead ourselves back on the path of Freedom – true Freedom, not the illusion of freedom that we have been living under.

Remember, there are more of us than there are of those in control. We can work in "secret" just as the darkness has, but instead by reaching up through prayer and requesting help from above. Our weapons of choice should be Love, Light, Forgiveness, Compassion, Understanding, and Prayer. These are all intangible weapons that will do no harm to anyone.

The ultimate agenda of these Secret Societies is to bring about a New World Order (One World Government). Their plan is that all countries would be ruled by the Dark Cabal, and we would have few or no rights at all. The intention would be to make us a slave society.

Please do not misunderstand what I am saying. Not all members of the "Secret Societies" are part of the Illuminati or Dark Cabal. Most are upstanding, loyal, law-abiding citizens. The structure is set up so that depending upon the level you have earned within the "Society" determines how much "secret" information you are able to have access to. Only very few members of the Secret Societies are able to have full access to all information.

This system is very manipulative. To move up the ranks of any of the Secret Societies, the leaders have to know that the member can be trusted. If there is any possibility that the member would not be loyal to the Society, the member would not have an opportunity to move up the chain of command.

HUMANS REGARDED AS FOOLS

The Dark ETs think of humans as fools. We react through FEAR. The acronym for FEAR is False Evidence Appearing Real. They have used this against us throughout our many lifetimes. They create a problem, expose it to us in a fearful manner, usually through the media; we react to this false evidence that appears to be real, and then we give them our permission to create a solution.

CONTROL STRATEGY – PROBLEM/REACTION/SOLUTION

Those at the top of these Secret Societies create a problem that causes an emotional reaction in humanity and which requires immediate attention. We demand a solution.

Then they create a solution for this problem they created, which seems to satisfy the need, but ultimately serves their own dark purposes. We are none the wiser. Smart, huh!

I now understand why they think of us as "fools" - their control strategy is ingenious. We are like puppets and willingly follow their lead which is NOT in our highest best interest. We are like putty in their hands to mold and shape us to their needs and if we resist then death do us part.

SWINE FLU

One example of creating a problem in need of an immediate solution would be the Swine Flu. It was created in a laboratory; the media announced that it would reach epidemic proportion. This created a reaction – panic/fear.

The solution was to create a vaccine. How this vaccine served the purposes of the Dark Cabal and not humanity was that the vaccine contained nanotechnology and when injected into the human, released a mind control substance.

Once again, the Beings of Light through the Galactic Federation of Light neutralized the nanotechnology contained in the vaccines. Once the Dark Ones realized that it was ineffective, they recalled the vaccine.

KILLING US SLOWLY

The Dark Cabal are more than happy to provide us with a solution as we have given them permission to slowly kill us through the poisons that are being put in our vaccines/medicines, food, water, air, soil, etc.

This is why it is so important that we wake up NOW and take control back and finally eliminate the darkness which no longer serves a purpose on Earth. It is time for us to finally experience Heaven on Earth – the original Plan of God through our Free Will decisions.

Always keep in mind there are more of "us" than there are of "them." It's time to show them we are NOT fools.

GLOBAL WARMING

Another problem created by the Dark Forces is that of Global Warming. This is NOT a problem in reality. It is only a problem if we listen to what the Dark Forces are telling us in order to create a fear-based society around the world. The more they can keep us in fear-mode, the lower our vibration will be, and the more control they will have over us. It also delays our Ascension Process.

Even though it appears that the planet is "warming" up, this is part of a natural process and something that the Earth has gone through during different times of its history. Don't panic. Know that the planet is protected as we are. It would be extremely helpful if our leaders would not tamper with the natural flow of things with their experimental weather technologies.

UNITED NATIONS

One of the most important solutions to a major 20th century problem was the creation of the United Nations. The United Nations is a front organization established after World War II to ensure that another world war would not happen. Unfortunately, the "real" mission was to bring countries together under one umbrella organization in support of the One World Government.

Oddly enough the United Nations has authority to step in and take military control over a region or country which is going against the plan of a One World Government. This seems contradictory to the reason it was originally created.

The creation of the UN was a first phase in establishing a One World Government. The next step was the creation of the European Union. This was a test and if it worked then the North American Union would be next with the uniting of the United States, Canada and Mexico. Talks regarding this Union began under President George W. Bush's administration. I'm not sure if this plan has been put on hold or is at another stage at this point.

If the European Union and the North American Unions went according to plan, then they would join forces and become one union. There are also plans to organize the South American Union, the African Union, and Asian Union. Then all these separate unions would unite and the One World Order (Government) would be established with one dictator (with a dark agenda) to lead the entire world.

It's really scary to realize how close they are to making this a reality. Again, people, it's time for us to WAKE UP and do our part whatever that part may be.

WHO'S TO BLAME?

NO ONE is to blame. Everything is happening as part of the Divine Plan for Earth. It was a Great Experiment to see how we would react if given a choice called Free Will. No doubt about it, darkness is a powerful force, but when LIGHT over-shadows the darkness, it can't help but be rendered useless.

When you take away the elements of Compassion, Sympathy, Empathy, Forgiveness, and Love, it is very easy for the Dark Ones to commit the acts of cruelty, murder, torture, terrorism, etc., as these acts only provide a great sense of power and control for them.

We all have an aspect of darkness within our heart. In each situation we can choose to follow the path of darkness or that of Light. It is our Free Will decision. It appears to be natural to follow the path of darkness when we are in a lower vibration. However, through the process of evolution and when we reach higher levels of vibration, it is much easier to follow the path of Light.

Humanity, as a whole, has gotten too lazy especially with our politicians. We expect them to protect and watch out for us when, in fact, all they are doing is protecting and watching out for themselves. We, all of humanity, not just Americans, need to make the officials of our governments responsible/accountable for what does not serve our highest and best interest during their watch. We need to insist upon banishing all the secret meetings and keeping us in the "dark" as to what is really going on. We need to know the truth and have a say in the actions taken to resolve national issues. War is no longer an option for resolving the disputes of the world.

Many of these Secret Societies were formed by the governments of the world. Ever wonder why it is necessary for so many aspects of the U.S. Government to be "secret" to the point where the leaders would use fatal force if anyone tried to set foot into these off limit places in the U.S.?

Over the years, many of these so-called Secret Societies were banned from operation. However, they went "underground" and became stronger than ever and are still operating today.

NATIONAL SECURITY AGENCY & THE AGE OF BIG BROTHER

The NSA (National Security Agency) was founded in 1952. It was originally intended as a technical surveillance system on certain individuals who were perceived as a national security threat. However, it has expanded to a full-fledged spy operation, not only on all U.S. citizens, but other world leaders as well.

This agency has created yet another opportunity to operate in "secret," keeping the public unaware of what is going on behind the scenes. I believe the reason they felt it necessary to spy on all U.S. citizens was due to the Awakening and Ascension processes that are taking place on Earth very rapidly now. They needed to know how many of us were aware of the "secrets."

Ed Snowden who was a contractor for the NSA leaked details to the press regarding extensive internet and phone surveillance by the U.S; again, not only of U.S. citizens, but also leaders of other countries.

Ed Snowden faces espionage charges, but I think he deserves a medal. What many people don't know is that Ed Snowden had a Soul contract to reveal this information (as a whistle blower) to the public because it was time for us to wake up and KNOW what is going on behind the scenes. However, when this information was released to the media, there was little or no reaction from the American citizens – no outbursts or demands that it be stopped. Recently the court ruled that the NSA can continue its surveillance on all U.S. Citizens. This was no surprise to me. The Illuminati influences the judiciary system. Maybe if "we" had spoken up louder, the outcome would have been different.

Many other individuals in physical form have Soul contracts as "whistle blowers," but may not follow through out of fear for their own life. It wouldn't do any good to put these individuals in a type of "witness" protection program, as the enemy for them would be those who were supposed to be protecting them.

I don't have anything to hide, but it is disturbing to know that through surveillance by our government, there are records being stored regarding every aspect of our daily life – they know everything about us, who we are with, who we are talking to, and what we are doing. The NSA has access not only to all our email correspondence, but our internet searches and phone records as well. For someone who lives in a "free" country, it doesn't seem as if all the spying is necessary.

Also, think of the amount of our tax dollars that is being spent on this surveillance project. We could probably afford free healthcare for all U.S. citizens by stopping this project alone or only keeping track of "suspected" criminals, not every citizen.

The NSA seemed to have no clues about the 9/11 attack on the Twin Towers. However, several individuals later came forward to say that they had reported to government officials the possibility of an attack on the U.S.

It appears that our leaders were either sleeping or turned a deaf ear to what was being reported in order to put us on alert. OR as many have speculated, our own government had a hand in orchestrating this event to move into a Third World War for depopulation purposes (see chapter 16) and a step closer to the One World Government.

The potential for abuse of this surveillance project far outweighs any protection it could offer.

I was watching a TV program on the History Channel and the individual (I don't remember the name) said: "Whenever you hear 'for your own good' from the government, know that you are about to lose money or freedom or possibly both."

The age of "Big Brother" has only just begun. We need

to stand up and protect ourselves, our rights and our freedom. We now know that the ball is in our court.

The Washington Post conducted an investigation titled
"A Hidden World, Growing Beyond Control." Some of
their findings were:

- After years of unprecedented spending and growth,
  the result is that the system put in place to keep the
  United States safe is so massive that its effectiveness
  is impossible to determine.
- 1,271 government organizations and 1,931
  private companies work on programs related
  to counterterrorism, homeland security and
  intelligence in about 10,000 locations across the
  United States.
- An estimated 854,000 people hold top-secret
  security clearances.
- Many security and intelligence agencies do the same
  work, creating redundancy and waste. For example
  51 federal organizations and military commands
  track the flow of money to/from terrorist networks.

It would appear that our tax dollars would be better spent on hiring experts to recognize all the waste and
duplicity and take steps to cut back where necessary instead
of just hiring more and more individuals to work under the
veil of secrecy.

The U.S. Intelligence Committee consists of 17 different organizations, each operating under a veil of secrecy. It

appears that one agency doesn't know what the others are doing and, in my opinion, this would lead to an extremely disorganized, uninformed operation, which our tax dollars are paying approximately $75 billion annually.

The NSA, the CIA, and the FBI are three of the major government organizations working with a dark agenda. While darkness is a force to be reckoned with, it can be defeated very easily through a mass consciousness of positive, loving, caring Light humans.

Again, it is our (humanity's) responsibility to stand up, and more importantly, speak up when something is being implemented on our behalf that we feel is not right. Even though it is our government telling us that they are doing it for our own good, or for our protection, we have the right to say "NO!" We can do this individually, or through petitions to our government representatives, or through groups of like-minded individuals. It is important that we do something instead of accepting what is handed to us whether we like it or not. The more accepting we are, the more rights that we have will be taken away.

Chapter 9

ILLUMINATI

The dictionary definition of Illuminati is:

1) Any of various groups claiming special religious enlightenment.
2) Persons who are or who claim to be unusually enlightened.

The Illuminati falls under #2 – Persons who "claim" to be enlightened. They would like us to believe they are the Illumined or Enlightened Ones. The Illuminati referred to in this book is NOT a group of individuals who are enlightened spiritually. They are "endarkened" if such a word exists.

There is nothing enlightened about individuals who feel they need to operate in secret, who feel that they are far superior to the majority of humanity and do not abide by the laws which they make for us, and who control the masses even to the point where they eliminate (murder) individuals who will not follow their lead or keep their secrets. To me this spells Darkness with a capital "D."

Members of the Illuminati developed their psychic abilities, worked through their Ego Self (instead of their Higher God Self) and ultimately misused their God-given gifts for the purpose of controlling all aspects of life on Planet Earth.

The Illuminati consists of 13 Papal Bloodline Families. They are at the top of the pyramid right below the Reptilians. This small group of individuals owns almost half of the wealth on Earth and increasing their share daily. Since there are approximately 7.5 billion people on Earth at this time, it does not leave too much for the rest of us. I guess if they have most of the money, it only makes sense that they would be calling the shots. Unfortunately, these shots are hurting humanity, not helping.

Nothing of major importance happens without their approval. They are also known as the Ruling Elite, Global Elite, and make up a sizable portion of the Shadow Government.

The Illuminati has a self-serving agenda to amass the majority of wealth, to take over control of the world and to eliminate much of humanity, using the balance for slave purposes. Their belief is those who own the wealth have the power.

The Illuminati is made up of the very wealthy – the

elite. Before I go any further, I am not talking about all wealthy people being part of the Illuminati network. This is a very close knit group of 13 families and approximately 85 family members. There is a good possibility that not all members of these families are aware of the secret activities of this group. It was once a very Secret Society but is not so secret anymore.

The Illuminati is not a group or Secret Society you can join. It is all about being part of the 13 bloodline families and they keep these bloodlines as pure as possible through inbreeding. In other words they marry their own kind.

Individuals can be associated with the Illuminati through membership in a variety of other Secret Societies, but unless you are born into the 13 families, you are not considered a member of the Illuminati.

The term Illuminati is used loosely for several different groups who are operating secretly (behind the scenes), yet having global power over all areas of the world's finances and population. It's like the brand name Kleenex, being referenced for all other brands of tissue.

The 13 families, who hold most of the wealth on Earth, needed individuals to carry out their wishes. These individuals needed to be loyal and not divulge the behind the scenes happenings. Over many years, several so-called Secret Societies were formed in order to oversee certain areas of life on Earth.

The Illuminati is also referred to as the Secret, Invisible or Shadow Government. Those who "work" for the Illuminati, but are NOT "family" are referred to as the Dark Cabal. They are placed in organizations/corporations in positions of power in order to oversee that business is carried out according to the wishes of the Illuminati.

The Illuminati/Dark Cabal uses the tools of fear, separation, greed and manipulation to control humanity. They have taken over control of all major aspects of life, such as:

Most Governments of the World

Financial/Banking Institutions

All Military Branches

Religious Organizations (Vatican #1)

Large Corporations

Education

Scientific/Medical Research

Pharmaceutical/Hospitals/Doctors

Media

Stock Market

Entertainment including Hollywood & Music Industry

Judiciary System

Secret Societies

Mind Control Programs

Contracts with ETs (Reptilians/Greys)

That Just About Covers Everything!

Many (not all) of our world leaders are members of the Illuminati. Some of the Illuminati members are Reptilians clothed in physical human bodies, while others work behind the scenes in the "shadows."

The Illuminati and Dark Cabal claim to worship Lucifer as their God. After all, the name Lucifer means "The Light Bearer" so they consider themselves evolved enlightened beings, or at least want us to believe they are "superior." However, I believe the Illuminati invented the character Satan and that is who they are worshipping. Satan was their own creation who was blamed for the activities carried out by the Dark Ones.

The logo or trademark for the Illuminati is the pyramid with the capstone missing and the all-seeing eye on top. This mark appears on the U.S. dollar bill. Some believe this is the mark of evil. Possibly this is why many humans perceive money as the root of all evil! However, as stated in the King James Version of the Bible – 1 Timothy 6:10 – *"For the love of money is the root of all evil; which while some coveted after, they have erred from the faith, and pierced themselves through with many sorrows."* It's the love (or greed) for money that is the root of all evil, NOT money.

The power and wealth of the Illuminati increases with each generation. They reincarnate into the same families/ bloodlines and keep themselves as pure as possible through inbreeding. In this way, they are born into wealth each lifetime and keep their mission alive of controlling and dominating the world. It appears the saying with regard to wealth that "you can't take it with you" is true, but you can arrange to be born into it over and over again when creating your Life Plan for each lifetime.

Only very few members of the Illuminati know all the details of the Plan. The rest of the members operate on a need-to-know basis. The individuals who are in the know are at the top of the organization. In this way they can be assured that their secrets will not be revealed. If individuals speak out about the truth of what is going on, they can be easily "eliminated." That is definitely incentive to remain quiet.

Humanity has become slaves to the Illuminati without even realizing it. Personally I had no idea this was the case until I started researching and receiving information for this book. It is very obvious now that I am aware of the strategy they used in order to become in control of the population on Earth. It really is ingenious and we played our part by allowing them to take control. We have that same power to take control out of their hands and put it into the hands of the "People."

The driving force for the Illuminati is power, money, and control to be able to dominate all of humanity once they succeed with their plan of a New World Order/One World Government.

The Illuminati has been working toward a secret plan for several thousand years. These families can be traced back to over 4,000 years ago.

I am happy to be a human on Earth at this time, and I am especially proud to be an American. I also do not hold judgment or resentment toward our leaders whether they are Republican or Democrat, as I know they are only figureheads who are also being manipulated by the Shadow Government. If they do not follow the lead which is given to them, they could meet with sudden death. Look at what happened to President John F. Kennedy when he made his own decisions as to what was best for the United States. His own son told me a surprising story.

A MESSAGE FROM JOHN F. KENNEDY, JR.

John F. Kennedy, Jr. casually mentioned (he did not make a formal announcement) that he was "thinking" of running for President, and he met with sudden death, which "appeared" to be an accident. I believe the powers-that-be knew if JFK, Jr. ran for president that he would definitely be elected and they would not be able to control him as they were not able to control his father. So it was quite convenient for him to meet with sudden death as well.

According to my Guides and the Akashic Records, the plane crash was not an accident – it was circumstances set up to make it appear as if it were an accident, when in fact it was a triple murder situation for which no one was held responsible.

I was meditating this (7/13/15) evening and the light in the room started to blink on and off (another method Spirit uses to get my attention). When I asked who was there, the response was John F. Kennedy, Jr. He had come to me while I was in church the previous day on Sunday, 7/12/15 to introduce himself and indicated that he would be coming forward with a quote for my book and that it would be filled with Light as his father's message had been.

Following is the quote I received from him:

It is with the greatest amount of pleasure that I inform everyone that I am doing just fine. I have found a way of fighting darkness from the Light, and it is much easier than trying to fight it in physical form. They (the Illuminati) are ruthless and have no conscience in how they get their plan to materialize. Therefore, the Galactic Federation of Light beings has banded together, and we see victory for humanity, however, not without humanity doing its part.

First, do not believe what the governments of the world tell you when they say they are looking out for you and only have your interests in mind. They only have their own interests in mind.

Second, reach up to the Light Beings who have been assigned to you to help you with your journey through life. If you do not ask for their intervention in your personal situations, they are not able (according to Universal Law) to step in and help. They are begging and pleading for humanity to reach up and ask for assistance no matter how minor the situation may be. Once individuals realize that the Light will set them free from darkness, then darkness will release the stronghold it now has on humanity.

As you know, there are many Light beings helping humanity on a major level. You have to deal with the smaller events, but you are not alone. They can help you, but you have to ask. It is not wrong to ask for help, but it is wrong to sit back and think that God is going to save you. You have to take steps in saving yourself by reaching up and asking; then they will come flooding in to do whatever they can.

Please know that my passing was unfortunate, however, it has turned into a blessing for me and many others who have passed as my father and I have – through the hand of the Illuminati, because they did not like that we did not take orders from them, that we had our own agenda which involved looking out for the citizens of the United States and, in turn, of the world.

This is what God intended for the creation of the United States of America. However, many things have been changed without your knowing. This will come to Light soon and they will have to answer to the people, and they definitely will not like being put in that position.

We applaud you for the effort you are making in getting word out so that individuals are able to help with the mission of bringing Heaven to Earth.

Thank you for this opportunity to provide my message in your book. You are an old Soul and have been a politician in the years when there was not so much corruption taking place on all levels. You wondered why you would be chosen to write such a book. It is to balance the rights with the wrongs going on in the world governments.

We all wish you much success with your mission and see that it will be successful in informing, not all of humanity, but those who need to see the Light of what has been and is going on. Your trust has been broken and promises have been broken. But the

world is on the brink of a new era – one filled with the things
that have been missing for quite some time.

God bless you in everything you do.
John F. Kennedy, Jr.
July 13, 2015

Two other individuals on the list Sananda gave me
about including a message in this book were Marilyn Monroe and Princess Diana.

Both ladies had come to me when I was not in a position to write their quote down, but said they came forward
to introduce themselves and promised to return later at a
more convenient time to give me their messages.

I kept waiting and reaching up and asking them to
come forward as I had to finish the writing so that I could
go to press quickly. No response, but I am familiar with
Spirit. Things are done in Divine time, not "my" time.

Finally after approximately six weeks, I was signaled by
Sananda that he had the two ladies with him, and they were
ready to give me their messages. Following are the messages I received from each of them.

A MESSAGE FROM MARILYN MONROE

I am so sorry for all the trouble I caused individuals that
were very kind to me, and I disrespected their kindness. So the
purpose of my wanting to put a quote in your book on Darkness
is because I was caught up in darkness during my career. It was
too much for me to handle so I resorted to taking drugs to help me
calm down and relax. In no time at all I was "hooked."

I was totally obsessed with getting on my next high. Many wonderful people tried to help me, but I just took advantage of them. While my death was definitely a murder, it was for the best. I had become a real nuisance and a threat to certain people and they wanted me out of the way. Unfortunately, it was not who you might think that had me eliminated – it was the Illuminati.

I give my love to all of humanity as I see from this perspective that things are really rough. You do not have a say in the workings of what goes on in your world. You have many wonderful Light Beings helping you such as the Archangels, Ascended Masters, Sananda, etc., but you need to take control back and free yourself from the Dark Ones who are making you sick and keeping you from being the Light Beings that you are meant to be. I love you!

Marilyn

God Bless You All

8/17/15

A MESSAGE FROM PRINCESS DIANA

It is with the utmost of respect that I come forward and tell my story. I was a common ordinary girl, and I did have a Soul Contract to be part of the Royal Family in England. However, it was not a comfortable place for me to be.

While I did get on drugs and also got "hooked," it was not my choice. It was decided for me in order for them to be able to mold me into who they wanted me to be. I was supposed to be waving and smiling at the public. Yes, they wanted the public to adore me because it made them look good as well. However, when I started to act out as a result of the drug use, I became a problem.

Long story short, the accident was not an accident, it was staged in order to release me. There was speculation that I was pregnant and that is why they wanted to get rid of me and it was not the truth. The truth is they were afraid that I would give the story, the real story of what goes on in the Palace, to the news media.

I had gotten off the drugs and had threatened to expose them for who they really were. I now know that I should not have done that, for that is the real reason I had to be eliminated.

I miss my boys, but I see that they have grown up to be fine young men, and I am proud of them. Kate is absolutely a doll, and I wish I could have been there for them. I would not have made the threat if I knew what the outcome was going to be. At least I am able to watch from up here and I am appreciative of that.

The good news is that the Beings of Light are in the process of "cleaning up" Planet Earth from the darkness, but please step in and do your part to help them. You will be amazed at what you are capable of doing if you band together.

From up here we are able to see the Light that you carry and it is bright. Thank you for allowing Marilyn and myself to have a voice in your book.

Love

Diana

8/17/15

Chapter 10

COMMITTEE OF 300

The British East India Company's Council of 300 created massive wealth as a result of selling opium to India and China. The Committee of 300 is an offshoot of the Council of 300.

The Committee of 300 is a group of global elite (not just British) with a secret plan to control the world. The plan for control was easy – whoever held the greatest amount of wealth would hold power/control over the entire planet. They have been amassing wealth at our (humanity's) expense for quite some time. This Committee works very closely with the Illuminati/Shadow Government.

The Committee of 300 seems to be our biggest enemy. It acts as the leader overseeing many other elite secret organizations, which include our world leaders. They are closely associated with the Illuminati and are sometimes referred to as the Illuminati. I assume that most, if not all, of the heads of the 13 Illuminati families are members of the Committee of 300 as well.

My Spirit Guides gave me an outline for this book and the outline indicated that certain well-known individuals would come forward with a quote for this book in order to clarify the "real" reason for their deaths. Their deaths were not as presented in the news media. I received three messages from Robin Williams and one from Michael Jackson.

A MESSAGE FROM ROBIN WILLIAMS

I was very saddened to hear the news of Robin Williams' passing on August 11, 2014. The news broadcast indicated that it was a suicide by hanging.

Shortly after his passing, I had a class scheduled to teach from my book, *Soul Releasement: Assisting Souls into the Light*, to a group at my church. Part of the agenda included giving the class time to connect with a deceased loved one's energy to determine if they were earthbound, in the Resting Area, or if they were in the Light. If earthbound or in the Resting Area, they had instructions to counsel their loved one's Soul to get them into the Light/Heaven.

During that time of the class, I would be sitting idle so I asked Jesus if Robin Williams' Soul was earthbound or in the Resting Area, as most Souls who commit suicide stay earthbound for fear that they will go to hell if they leave the Earth plane. Jesus said that Robin Williams' Soul was definitely earthbound. So I asked Jesus if He could bring Robin's Soul energy to me for counseling during the class in order to help him arrive in the higher dimensions. Jesus agreed.

As I connected with Robin's energy, his "voice" in my head was exactly as it sounded in real life, except that he was extremely serious – absolutely NO humor. I attributed this to the fact that there is nothing funny about suicide and he must have been in an awful frame of mind in order to end his life.

I counseled him on the importance of forgiving, not only those who had hurt him, but more importantly, forgiving himself. I explained that he had a wonderful escort to the Light (Jesus) and that he needed to retrieve his sense of humor so that he could tell jokes to God about Jesus. I only got a slight smile from him on that comment. Anyway, Jesus escorted him to the Resting Area and worked with him to help him release the negativity he was holding onto. In a very short period of time, he was escorted to the Light from the Resting Area by Jesus.

While at a conference in the Chicago area, a neighbor vendor (without knowing that I had assisted Robin Williams' Soul to the Light) asked me if I knew anything about his death. I told her that with the help of Jesus, I assisted his Soul to the Light. She said that she had heard he was murdered and did not commit suicide. Initially, I was surprised to hear this piece of information, but said I would check with Jesus when I had a chance to meditate.

During the conference I was too busy and too tired at the end of the day to meditate so I decided I would wait until I returned home to peace and quiet. However, before I had an opportunity to meditate and check on this information about Robin Williams being murdered, I was signaled by massive goose bumps running up and down my body (this is Spirit's way of getting my attention when they want to communicate). When I asked if someone from Spirit needed to talk with me, I was informed that it was Robin Williams who had come to explain what actually happened regarding his passing.

Following is what he had to say:

The Shadow Committee that oversees the entertainment industry had asked me to step aside that my reign was up. They asked that I step aside quietly or "they" would bring me down. I thought that they meant they would try to smear my reputation by fabricating lies, so I did not pay attention to these threats.

The symptoms of Parkinson's were brought about by medicine prescribed for another condition. What was indicated on the label of the prescription was not what it contained. This medication made me delirious, which was supposed to create an image that I was losing my mind in order to discredit me.

I stopped taking the medication because I knew it was causing my hallucinations. I threatened that I was going to expose them for who they were. This caused the "Committee" to step up the process of silencing me, and it appears to have worked.

During our conversation I asked Robin who "they" were and he indicated the Committee. In my research of the Secret Societies operating under the umbrella of darkness, I found the Committee of 300. I am not sure if this is the Committee Robin spoke about, it is just a possibility. I also asked Robin how was he murdered and he indicated that "they" smothered him; then staged the hanging to avoid an investigation of murder.

Robin also indicated that he has connected with others from the entertainment industry, who have been eliminated in similar ways as he was – namely, John Lennon and Michael Jackson.

Even though Robin had given me a quote for this book shortly after his arrival on the Other Side, he came forward while I was in Sedona and asked if he could add more information.

Following is what he had to say:

No jokes about Jesus! I forgive those who felt it was necessary to do me in. While I understand the reason why now, I didn't at the time it was happening. However, America is a free country. We were supposed to have had the opportunity to say whatever we wanted without worrying about harm plaguing us.

I am proud to be included in this book on Darkness as it is time for all to know what is going on behind their backs with smiley faces as a mask of all the dirty deals being made against humanity. If I were there now, I would have written a book exposing what little I knew of the Cabal "organization."

The U.S. is one of the least "free" countries in the world. Freedom and rights are being abused and taken away daily and no one seems to be doing anything about it, and if they try, then they are either punished, made ill, or killed. If one method doesn't work, the ultimate sacrifice is death and this is NOT funny – not a laughing matter as I projected in my routines. It would have been better for me to write a serious non-fiction book and release it without releasing bits and pieces in the form of humor. Because I was using humor as a tool to release the TRUTH, no one took me seriously. So my author friend (Barbara), I applaud you for putting into words what humans need to know, and hopefully they will do their part in eliminating the darkness from their lives.

P.S. Jesus said it would be all right for me to make jokes about him. He likes a good laugh. Laughter helps to raise our vibration.

I send my love to you and all who miss me. I certainly miss my family, friends, and fans – the three F's.

While I was in the process of typing the above message from Robin, I received the full body goose bump signal that someone from Spirit wanted to communicate with me. It was Robin again and he had more information he wanted to include. Following is what he had to say on this day – May 27, 2015:

I thank you for helping me "find" my sense of humor. As you know, after my death I was in no mood to make jokes. However, Jesus is such a wonderful Being of Light. He has assured me that Heaven is where I was made and laughter is one of the best medicines for whatever ails you.

I have fully recuperated from the trauma of my death and wanted to share with you, and all who read your book, that it is important to live a good, clean, laughter-filled life, as stress, anger, and all the other negative emotions have no place in Heaven. You can't get into Heaven if you carry the negativity with you upon death. Shed them as a snake sheds its skin even before death.

It is really hard to explain because Heaven is a word that most people think is unexplainable and it is. Take the most perfect glorious day you could ever imagine and multiply that by 1,000 and that is what it is like up here in Heaven. I thank you for helping me to understand that I needed to go to the Resting Area in order to release the negativity I was hanging onto.

The Resting Area was not a bad place, but it was sure good to get out of there and brought to where I am now – the Fourth Dimension. I am with many others who I knew while on Earth. Some are from the entertainment circle I was in, but others are family, friends and fans I never had an opportunity to meet. We are all together as one. No celebrities up here. We are all the same. That ego part of us is non-existent in Heaven. And if anyone tries to use their earthly ego, they are laughed at as if they were a comedian. I love it up here, but I truly miss my earthly life as well. I have been given an opportunity to make a new Life Plan, but I think I will wait awhile before returning. It feels too good up here to leave it behind just yet.

Again, I thank you for this opportunity to express myself in your book and I do feel honored to be able to call you "my friend!" God Bless You and Everyone!

Robin Williams
5/27/15

POKING FUN AT THE SHADOW GOVERNMENT

After receiving Robin's quote as to how and why he died, I wondered if any other comedians who poked fun at the Shadow Government died in a similar way. In my search, George Carlin's name came up and sure enough it was speculated that it was no "coincidence" that he died of chest pains a few months after his show about what was going on behind the scenes of our government went viral on YouTube, and only 5 days after it was announced that he would be receiving the Mark Twain Prize for American Humor.

While I don't believe everything I read on the internet, if it sounds plausible, I reach up and check with my Spiritual Guidance for the truth. It was confirmed by Jesus/Sananda that George Carlin's death was the work of the Dark Cabal. Because of his worldwide popularity he was touching on a subject that would get intelligent people thinking and "they" could not afford to be exposed.

In another incident, I was doing a reading for a wife, whose husband had committed suicide. I do many readings of this nature. However, I kept getting the feeling that it was not a suicide – it was murder. Since I was not being told by my Spiritual Guidance that it was NOT suicide, I kept my personal feelings to myself. The husband was earthbound (which is very normal under the circumstances) and during the session, I requested an escort from the Heavenly Realm to take his Soul to the Light. Jesus/Sananda came forward as the escort.

After my session with the wife was over, I meditated and asked Jesus/Sananda whether or not the entity he escorted to the Light was murdered or if his death was, in fact, a suicide? His response was "No! It was murder, but it will never come to Light." I now know why I was getting that impression, but did not reveal it to my client. During the counseling session she was able to accept that she could not have done anything to prevent his death. The burden was lifted so I was not being guided to throw another burden at her. When she told me what her husband's profession was, I understood why it was a murder staged as a suicide.

As humans, we wonder why God would let such things happen. The answer is Free Will! It is our responsibility to STOP such activity here on Earth. We are its keepers and we are remiss in our duties. We have placed ourselves in the hands of individuals who do not have our highest best interest in their hearts or minds.

They are self-serving. Again, please do not get me wrong, not all politicians or leaders of large corporations are corrupt. However, the closer we get to God on our journey through life, the better we are able to "see" the good from the bad. This is part of the enlightenment process and this is what the Illuminati are trying to keep us from reaching. It is our God-given right. It is the reason we are having this human experience – to become enlightened.

A MESSAGE FROM MICHAEL JACKSON

During my visit to Sedona, my friend invited me to attend a meditation meeting at one of her friend's home. This was an absolutely wonderful event. The energy was extremely high. During the meditation, Michael Jackson came forward and indicated that sometime during my stay in Sedona he would like to provide a quote for my book about his passing. I was thrilled as he was also on the list that Sananda had given me of individuals who would be providing information.

Following is the message Michael Jackson provided:

First of all, I would like to let everyone know that I NEVER, NEVER, NEVER molested children who stayed at Neverland Ranch with me. It was that I never had an opportunity to be and act as a child so I took the opportunity to have that experience with children. I enjoyed their company much more than they enjoyed mine. I believe some of them thought I was 'crazy' the way I acted, but I was using the opportunity to have fun and play.

Once I became rich and famous, I had the illusion that I could do anything and it would be accepted. But NEVER, NEVER, NEVER did I hurt children. I loved them too much. I wanted to enrich their lives and to help them have advantages that they otherwise would not be able to have. I NEVER, NEVER, NEVER even thought about taking advantage of them sexually or in any way.

Next I would like to share why I died. It certainly wasn't a natural death. I was sick and tired of the Committee trying to rule my every move and every word that came out of my mouth. I thought if I made them nervous thinking that I might divulge their secret existence to the public they would back off and leave me alone. I told them if they left me alone and didn't try to control me, I would also leave them alone. I had no idea that I would become a threat to them and it would be necessary for me to be "deleted" from human existence.

Things were always kept pretty much secret regarding the goings on in the entertainment industry. I do have to admit that this same Committee that extinguished me was responsible for my popularity. They supported and promoted me throughout my career. However, they owned me as well and that is something I no longer wanted to tolerate.

I miss all of my fans, friends and family, but the good part is that I am able to keep track of them from up here. I couldn't while I was in the Resting Area, but now I have complete access to knowing what they are doing and how they are doing. It is important to me to know that, even though there was some turmoil at the beginning of my passing, everything will work out for the best soon.

I want to apologize to anyone whom I might have offended or hurt during my stay on Earth. I am truly sorry for I see now the error of my ways with certain people. I lacked tolerance and that was a lesson I was there to learn.

I miss everyone, but I ask God to send you His blessings on a regular basis. I part now by saying I LOVE you – I LOVE everyone! Love is such a precious gift. Please do your part in sending Love to each other and also to Planet Earth!

Michael Jackson

5/7/15

It is appalling to think that this is going on in our world. Since much of humanity is awakening and feeling or knowing that things are NOT right, I believe we will get on the right track very soon and by banding together, we can make our leaders responsible for their actions and make them abide by the same rules they put in force for our "benefit."

Chapter 11

THE BILDERBERG GROUP

The Bilderberg Group is made up of very powerful and very wealthy individuals mostly (two-thirds) from Europe and the balance from the United States and Canada. The group was founded in 1954 and received its name "Bilderberg" because its first annual meeting was held at the Bilderberg Hotel in the Netherlands.

Their annual private conference consists of 120 to 150 political leaders and experts from industry, finance, academia, and the media.

The Bilderberg Group invites only the heads of the major media corporations to their meetings, however, they are not to report what is discussed in these meetings. They are sworn to secrecy. I believe that, in order to control the media and have them cooperate in ONLY reporting what is spoon-fed to them, it would be necessary to let them be part of the "secret" plans.

Even though many of the leaders of the top media organizations are members of The Bilderberg Group and attend the meetings, very little if anything is ever reported in the news. These are highly secret meetings. Again, their main mission is to assist in the preparation of a One World Government/New World Order, a global military force through the United Nations, as well as a unified church and monetary system all under their direction.

They take credit for the single Euro currency. They seem to have absolute control over the national and international media. However, our local/community media who report only the local news are not under their direct control. They report the news from local authorities and that is usually the truth. However, if the local media report on national or international news, they report only what has been given to them from the national/international sources.

Therefore, when The Bilderberg Group chooses a location for their annual meeting, all the staff (top to bottom) of that particular hotel is sworn to secrecy regarding anything that has to do with their meeting, including the guests attending. They are threatened not only with loss of their job, but never being able to work in their country again.

Secret Societies exist by deception. Those at the top of the organization are aware of their real agenda, but lie to the members below by making them believe the organization stands for something good – a noble cause, such as with the Freemasons and Skull & Bones Secret Societies.

There is not as much known about The Bilderberg Group as there is about the Committee of 300 and the Illuminati. Maybe that is because they only meet once a year in order to discuss and update the agenda for a One World Government.

Chapter 12

SHADOW GOVERNMENT

The Shadow Government is an accumulation of individuals from the top three Secret Societies. They are not in elected positions, but are making the decisions for those who are in office to carry out. Most of the time, these decisions are not for humanity's safety and protection, but more to lead us into a One World Government position.

Unfortunately, those who are part of the Shadow Government are being directed by the Dark Reptilians. One of the areas they have taken over and have full control of is the presidential elections in the United States.

SHADOW GOVERNMENT – ELECTIONS

While many are aware that our government officials lie, slander the opposition, and hardly ever keep their campaign promises, many are not aware that it doesn't matter who is elected (we the voters don't have any control over who is elected), there is a secret Shadow Government that controls all major events, not only in the United States, but on the entire Planet including who is elected.

The individuals who are members of the Illuminati are the ones making decisions behind the scenes for those who have been placed or elected into high ranking positions around the world, such as Presidents, Prime Ministers, etc.

Remember, not too long ago, the ballot "chad" incident during the election of George W. Bush. What a coincidence that happened in the state of Florida where Jeb Bush (his brother) was Governor. My guides have indicated that was a "fixed" election as the Shadow Government wanted George W. Bush in office, not Al Gore.

The Shadow Government has been in charge for many hundreds of years, even before the U.S. was established as a country to break away from the British. Their plan is to amass further wealth and power in order to be able to control the "people."

The Shadow Government has control over who is elected, all major media networks, the banking and economic systems, education and entertainment industries, health and pharmaceutical industries and all large corporations. It controls the wars that take place, such as the Russian, French, and American Revolutions, the U.S. Civil War, and World Wars I & II. Their plan was to perpetuate a Third World War mainly for depopulation purposes, but also to amass more wealth and to ultimately take control of the Planet. Fortunately for humanity the Beings of Light have intervened.

ELECTORAL VOTING

At least since 1913 (possibly before), all U.S. Presidents have been chosen by the Illuminati. This is due to the Electoral Voting system. I believe it is very easy to manipulate the Electoral Voting system and, according to my Guides, the reason it was put into operation was for the purpose of being able to implement the desired outcome. I think it is fascinating the hype that is generated on Election Day/Night watching the different states tally up their votes to see the outcome of the election.

First of all, a decision is made by the Illuminati as to who is their selection to be the next President. It has nothing to do with popular vote by the citizens of the United States. It has everything to do with the bloodline of the individual – whether or not they are connected to the Illuminati and will follow the direction of the "Shadow Government."

They do everything within their power to see that their choice of candidate wins the election. This is usually accomplished through the media. Remember all the mudslinging done during the campaign speeches? We weren't hearing what the candidate was going to do to make life better for the people, but how bad their opponent was.

When the public voiced their disgust about the way the campaigns were being run, an attempt was made to clean up the negativity, but it readily bounced back to the mud-slinging and back-stabbing campaigns again.

It is the responsibility of the media to try and sway the vote to the candidate of their choice. Another tactic to get their candidate elected is through cheating such as what happened with the ballots in Florida with George W. Bush winning over Al Gore. Again, according to my guidance, this was fixed in order for George W. Bush to get into office. The Illuminati needs to have leaders who will follow their directions.

Finally, as I have mentioned, they have the ability to manipulate the electoral votes.

Worst case scenario is that none of the above methods work, and their choice of candidate does not win. No problem, they always have a backup plan. Since they sponsored/funded both parties during the election process to create the illusion that it is an open and fair campaign (they like to entertain us and continue the illusion of Free Will), the actual winner is under obligation to follow the wishes of the Illuminati once in office. If this does not happen, then they can expect to fall victim to the same fate as President John F. Kennedy.

Chapter 13

MAJOR CONSPIRACY THEORIES & UFOS

When more than one person knows a "secret," it's very hard to keep it a "secret." The TV show *Conspiracy Theories with Jesse Ventura* has brought many secrets to the surface. The History Channel on TV has done due diligence in exposing many of the world's secrets. The Internet has several articles by many different individuals giving their perspective on some of these major conspiracy theories. Also, our Spirit Guides are downloading information to individuals regarding some of these mystery events in order to bring the TRUTH forward.

Following is only a very small sample of some of the major secrets, which have been exposed, but are still being denied:

UFO RECOVERED AT ROSWELL, NEW MEXICO IN JULY 1947

The U.S. government has denied that it was a UFO that crashed with Extraterrestrials on board. The government claimed that it was a top secret research balloon that crashed. It is believed that the reason they denied a UFO encounter was to protect us. It would be too fearful to be told UFOs exist and it might create panic throughout the U.S.

While that's a very logical and noble explanation, my personal opinion is that they kept the truth from us because they were working (in secret) with ETs. The government and members of the Secret Societies were receiving valuable information, and their fear was that, if the general populace also had the ability to work with the ETs, the Secret Societies would definitely lose control.

PRESIDENT JOHN F. KENNEDY'S ASSASSINATION
DALLAS, TEXAS – NOVEMBER 22, 1963

The Warren Commission at the conclusion of their investigation of the President's assassination indicated that it was carried out solely by Lee Harvey Oswald. However, to this day, it is believed that the President's assassination was caused by our own government officials.

I found a quote by President John F. Kennedy which stated: *"Mankind must put an end to war before war puts an end to mankind."* I am sure he was aware of the plan for a World War III, which would create a massive depopulation effort by approximately 90% of humanity. The Powers-That-Be find it too hard to control 7.5 billion humans and would like to eliminate approximately 7 billion. Five hundred million is their more manageable target number. WOW, this is a very aggressive plan and the only way they could implement it would be through a Third World War. Fortunately, as I understand from our Light Leaders, a Third World War will NOT happen.

PRINCESS DIANA'S DEATH – AUGUST 31, 1997.

It is believed that she was murdered to avoid further scandal to the Royal Family of England. (See Princess Diana's message in the Illuminati section.)

9/11 TWIN TOWERS – SEPTEMBER 11, 2001.

It appears that the U.S. government was aware of this event before it happened and either allowed it to happen or created it themselves for the purpose of creating a legitimate reason to enter into a Third World War.

PEARL HARBOR – DECEMBER 7, 1941.

Again, it is speculated that President Franklin D. Roosevelt knew about the attack and allowed it to happen in order to be able to enter into a World War II with Hitler.

"SECRETS" VS. "INTERNAL LIE DETECTOR"

It's very hard to believe that the leaders of our world would allow such events to happen; however, when you look at it from the dark side of things, how could they not happen? One thinks of this type of activity being carried out by criminals, however, the Dark Cabal is under the radar when it comes to taking responsibility for their actions. This is the mission of the different Secret Societies – to keep their actions secret.

One of the benefits of reaching the Ascended Master level of vibration is that we become "lie" detectors. We don't have to hook someone up to a machine or technical device to determine if they are telling the truth. Our own God Self sends us signals from above to alert us not to believe all that we are being told or shown. It is important that we pay attention for these "all-knowing" signs from above are extremely valuable. We "automatically" KNOW the truth.

Unfortunately, people have been able to lie to us in the past and get away with it. However, it is more difficult to get away with it with the fully enlightened or ascended ones.

UFOS & A MESSAGE FROM JOHN LENNON

I believe the reason our government denied the existence of UFOs and ETs is because they were working with them and they didn't want us to be able to have the same power/ability that they had.

They did pretend that they "lied" in order to protect us. There again, is the phrase "for our own benefit." The real reason they kept the truth from us was for their own benefit, not ours. Therefore, because the truth has been hidden, and those who have had experiences and were brave enough to share were ridiculed and made to believe that they just imagined the encounter.

John Lennon's quote (below) regarding the real reason for his death tells how desperate our leaders are to keep UFO and ET existences under cover for their own benefit, not ours.

I had asked Jesus/Sananda for an outline regarding what He wanted me to include in this book. One of the topics was individuals who had been eliminated by the Dark Cabal and wanted to include the real reason behind their passing. John Lennon's name was on this list of individuals.

I was attending an event where a unique young man was making reference to John Lennon. While he was able to channel John's music, another individual would channel messages from John and relay those messages to him. During intermission, I asked this young man if he could provide me with the contact information for the individual who channeled the messages from John Lennon. I wanted to be able to get John's permission to put his story in my book. I was told to check with him later when the class was over.

During the second half of the program we had time to meditate, so I reached up and asked if John Lennon happened to be present. Much to my delight he was. When I asked his permission to put a quote in my book regarding his passing, he said: *"Your Guides have already cleared this with me."* Since I did not have paper/pen available to take his quote down at that time I assumed he would come forward at another time. A few weeks later, while in Sedona, Arizona with a friend, I received a great deal of channeled information for this book. John Lennon came forward with the following message:

The real story of my passing had to do with my experience with a UFO. This happened while I was in London (not the States). I was up real late one evening as I was composing a new song. Out my window I saw a bright stationary light in the distance. It was very distracting to my being able to concentrate on the song. So I decided to get in my car and see if I could go and find the source of this bright light. As I got near my car the light was now over me. As I looked up, it (the light) sucked me up as if it were a vacuum cleaner. The beings who were on this ship were able to communicate with me through thought (not words). They told me they came to warn and protect me as it was my destiny to make contact and work with them in this lifetime.

The reason they came was to let me know that the "Powers-That-Be" on Earth were not ready for this type of activity to become public knowledge.

I did work with them for several months, and it was such a wonderful experience that I decided to share it with my fans. I had hoped that they knew and loved me enough to know that I was not crazy. That it was a real experience and that ETs were working with many humans, especially the leaders of World Governments.

Somehow word got out to the politicians in both England and the United States and I guess the decision was made for them to silence me. There were "Men in Black" who visited me and warned that it would not be a good idea for me to continue telling individuals about my experience. At first they tried to make me believe that they were warning me in order to protect me, my image, and reputation. They said people would think I was crazy and that would be the end of my career.

I heeded their advice at first, but it became an overwhelming desire for me to share my experience so that if others were to have the same or similar experience, they would not feel that they were alone. Because I would not adhere to the warning from the "Men in Black," a contract was put out for me to leave Planet Earth completely. I will not say who it was that put the contract in force, but it is someone you would never think would be interested in whether I was considered crazy by the public or not. It was a government official, a member of the Illuminati. It wasn't until I arrived up here (in the Fourth Dimension) that I was able to see the real reason why my life had to end at that time. Because of my worldwide popularity I would have had a major influence on humanity, not only believing that ETs and UFOs exist, but that we can have contact with them.

The Illuminati/Dark Cabal was working with the Dark ETs/Reptilians/Greys. They were getting much of their war weapons technology from them and didn't want humanity to know they had the same ability. They wanted to keep this information secret and I came along and wanted to share it with the world. The only difference was that I had connected with the ETs/UFOs who were working from the perspective of Light – who wanted to help humans not hurt them.

So the story as shown in the news as to why I was shot was definitely not the real story. I had to be eliminated in order for the cabal to keep their secret that there is no such thing as ETs or UFOs. Well, there are many of you who know that they do exist, but for those of you who are not sure, I tell you they do exist, but if you want to make contact with them, make sure they are of Light and not of darkness.

I thank this writer for the opportunity to be able to tell my story. Please do not believe everything that is told to you by your government officials for they do not always want what's best for you. I sign off with Love, Peace, Joy and Blessings to all of you.

John Lennon

5/5/15

PART IV

REPTILIANS & GREYS

Chapter 14

REPTILIANS & GREYS

The Reptilian agenda is to create a New World Order – a world based on control and domination. They already have a stronghold of control on Earth through the Illuminati and all the Secret Societies. It is NOW our time to make sure that they do not dominate us. If we connect with our Heavenly Helpers and work together, we can take back control and live a life full of Love, Happiness, Abundance, and Peace.

Ever since the creation of Earth there have been extra-terrestrial (non-human) influences trying to take control of not only the Planet, but humanity as well.

The Reptilians, who have the ability to shape-shift, are the most dangerous to humanity. They are extremely intelligent (far beyond human intelligence) especially in the area of technology. They also carry a very strong warrior and ego-driven mentality. What they lack are the human positive emotions, such as Love, Compassion, Sympathy/Empathy, Forgiveness, and Spiritual Enlightenment.

Above the high level human Illuminati are the Dark Reptilians (some clothed in human bodies) who work together with their off-planet counterparts. Their goal is world domination or destruction. They are prepared for whatever way the pendulum swings. Of course, they would prefer domination and control, but they feel they can destroy humanity and the Earth if things don't work out as they would like.

While we may think of the Reptilians as looking like the reptiles we are familiar with from the animal kingdom, they do not operate in reptile-type bodies as that would be too awkward. Many either create their own "human" body or their energy can occupy or possess an already existing human body. The more powerful ones operate behind the scenes (from their own home base) in their energy bodies while keeping full control over what is happening on Earth. They believe they own Earth and all of its inhabitants and resources.

Again, their intelligence and technology skills are far beyond that of humans and this is why many world leaders have entered into contracts with these beings – to obtain their technological knowledge, especially when it comes to nuclear power and war weaponry. Since the Reptilians are military-oriented, they have been responsible for much of the war activities that have taken place on Earth to this day.

The negative ETs do not follow or obey the Universal Laws. They have spent much time in devising ways to control humans. After many failed attempts they became successful in altering DNA by implanting negative materialistic desires and self-doubt to cause us to believe that we had no power.

Our government (U.S.) has been working with the Dark Forces for many years. They have assisted us in the development of war weapons, and we have given them the ability to have their way with humanity for whatever purposes they desired.

There have been offerings of assistance from peaceful, loving ETs, but their help has been refused. In ancient history there have been many reports when humans made reference to Gods coming down from the sky to help teach us how to exist on Earth – the ways of Light.

Unfortunately, the Dark Forces knew what our government wanted and came forward to offer war technologies which would put us in a number one position militarily, and the answer to this offer was YES!

ETs have had a major role on Planet Earth for most of our existence. In the beginning the so-called good ETs came to Earth to help us in getting started. They were a part of the civilizations which made up both Atlantis and Lemuria.

ETs in one way or another have existed since Earth was first inhabited. Many different species have wanted to take over and control humanity. It seems that the Dark ETs were more determined and have taken control without our knowledge. The reason all of these different ETs have had the opportunity to mess with humans and our evolution process directly relates to the fact that we have Free Will.

After the destruction of Atlantis, the planetary vibrational level fell back into the Third Dimension from the Fifth Dimension. Quite a setback for humanity. Our downfall was perceived by "on-lookers" from other Dark Dimensions (specifically the Reptilian Dark Forces) that Earth was vulnerable for take over and so the Reptilians took control of Earth. Unfortunately, the human leaders of Earth are guided by these non-human Reptilians even though they may be operating in human bodies. Sad but true.

The Dark Reptilians are the most negative, evil beings in the Universe. They can take responsibility for all the evil events which have taken place during the history of our Planet. It is NOT a warm and cozy feeling to think our government officials are in "business" with these beings.

Many other species over the course of Earth's history tried to take control of humanity – Anunnaki, Archon, Orions, Draconians, Greys, Reptilians, etc. However, the Greys and Reptilians seemed to have the greatest effect on humanity as they worked with the humans who were members of the Illuminati – our world leaders.

After the fall of Atlantis, the Anunnaki (Dark Reptilians) took over control of humanity on Earth and not in a good way. The Anunnaki created a great deal of suffering through hatred, war, and control over humanity. They remained in control for approximately 13,000 years.

The Anunnaki evolved out of darkness and are now operating from Light. In the mid-1990's they joined The Galactic Federation of Light. They are no longer a threat to humanity.

These other worldly beings (Anunnaki) had a hand in changing our DNA, which set humanity backward along our spiritual path. Our strands of DNA were reduced from 12 to 2 and we are just now getting that straightened out. The 12 stands gave humanity the ability to connect and communicate with our Heavenly Helpers. By reducing our strands of DNA to only 2 made us more dependent upon those in "charge."

While the Reptilians are highly intelligent and extremely advanced technologically, they are not evolved spiritually. They are able to shape-shift and create a human body at will. However, mostly they work through humans in their invisible state.

Military power is of utmost importance to the Dark Reptilians.

Dark Reptilians believe that they have power over Earth because of their conquest of working with humans. Many of them are working members of the Illuminati and the Dark Cabal on Earth.

Reptilians and Greys have had the most involvement

and control over humanity. Some are disguised in human bodies. However, most operate from behind the scenes in the shadows. They have the ability to clone a body or they can possess a human body if it is compatible to their blood-line. Over the years they have interbred with humans to create these bloodlines with the ultimate purpose of being able to control humanity. They need the human hormone in their blood in order to be able to shape-shift and look like a human.

The Greys are responsible for the abductions which were taking place on Earth. It was an agreement made with our government and there was a time limit attached to this plan. However, as is normal when working with darkness, they did not honor their agreement and went far beyond the limit that was agreed upon. The Greys have also imple-mented some mind control programs for humans as we out number them and it is a way for them to stay in control.

Many ET species, including the Reptilians, have ge-netically modified the human body. The Reptilians wanted humans to be of a lesser nature in order to use us as slaves. The Sirians (ETs of Light) genetically modified humans to what we are today – so that we could evolve beyond the Reptilian Dark mentality and into the Light.

Reptilians are very highly advanced with technology, but void in Compassion and Spirituality. They act as ag-gressive warriors and keep the leaders of the world prone to engaging in wars or warlike activities. If a problem doesn't exist, they will manufacture one in order to have reason to enter into a war.

The Reptilian species have played a major role regarding darkness on Planet Earth. It is important to keep in mind that not ALL Reptilians are of darkness. Just as humans can operate under the umbrella of Light or darkness so can the Reptilians. However, since the subject of this book is Darkness, the Dark Forces are being brought to Light. Unfortunately, the Dark Forces have been told that the Light will "kill" them so they do everything in their power to fight the Light.

The Reptilians, who were operating from their spiritual (energy) bodies, have been banned from Earth as the time of darkness on Earth is over. Unfortunately, there are some who are still remaining – hiding out. However, the majority of the Reptilian species (and Greys) have been escorted off Planet Earth.

Unfortunately, those who occupy human bodies still remain. The Beings of Light are working with their Higher Selves on the Other Side to advise them of the importance of letting go of their dark ways and turning towards the Light. If they choose to stay in darkness, then their Souls will be "dissolved" through their Free Will choice.

Therefore, not immediately, but slowly we will see signs of improvement for all occupants of Planet Earth – even those who once were operating under the umbrella of darkness!

Chapter 15

CONTROLS PLACED ON HUMANITY BY THE REPTILIANS

Alteration of DNA

Religion

Materialism/Greed

While it is easy to place the blame on the ETs/Reptilians, we played our part in the scheme and allowed them to have the control they desired. They have altered our DNA, created incorrect belief systems, and encouraged us to desire materialism and called greed "a good thing."

ALTERATION OF DNA

They are responsible for altering our DNA in 3 ways that I am aware of:

1. Deactivating 10 of our 12 strands of DNA. We originally had 12 strands of DNA. This gave us the ability to connect with our spiritual advisors on the other side to help us along our journey on Earth. This deactivation caused us to believe we were "human," not spiritual beings, and it was much easier for them to control us.

2. They implanted self-doubt, which in turn, created the need to have someone in a position of authority to oversee all aspects of our life, such as a baby needs its mother in the early stages of life.

3. Through inter-breeding with human women, it gave them an opportunity in future lifetimes to occupy a physical human body more easily so they could fit in and hold positions of authority giving them even more control.

RELIGION

Believe it or not, the negative ETs are the ones who introduced organized religion and the belief in only ONE God, and that compared to God we were not worthy. Instead we should have been told the truth - that our purpose for being on Earth was to grow to higher spiritual levels in order to become co-creators with God. However, that would not have served the needs of the Dark Forces, as their mission was to enslave us. It seemed that everything we did, no matter how insignificant was considered a "sin." This type of thinking suppressed our spiritual growth, and this was their intent. Through religion they have exercised a certain amount of control over us in the name of God!

Instead of going within and connecting with our God-Self, we turned ourselves over to the religious leaders for answers. If we did not conform to the rules/laws of our particular religion, it was possible that we could be thrown out of the church. This was a form of punishment.

Many enlightened beings came to Earth (Abraham, Buddha, Jesus, Mohammed, etc.) to show humanity the way of and to God – our purpose for being here. It is only now that much of humanity has awakened. The Reptilians have been in control for so long, that without the help of the Light Beings, we are not able to break free of the hold they have on us. So reach up! Reach up high and request assistance for all of humanity to be freed from the stronghold that we have allowed darkness to put upon us.

Religion is not evil because it was created under the umbrella of darkness. Many good things have resulted due to our belief in a higher power (God). It has brought more comfort to individuals who were suffering with life's challenges. The truth is that the dark beings distorted the truth of God's word in order to keep us from knowing who we really are and our purpose for being on Earth. The teachings they presented were an effort to keep us in fear, poverty, separation consciousness, and under their control.

I don't expect many of you to believe that Jesus does not favor any religion, especially Christianity, but He doesn't. It is filled with dark teachings that are supposedly based on His teachings. Very little of what is contained in the Bible is part of Jesus' teachings. In the Fourth Century, Roman Emperor Constantine decided to create the Bible. Constantine's reason for doing so was because Jesus still had many followers, and he wanted to gain control of those followers through the creation of the Bible.

Again, believe it or not, Lucifer had a hand in including whatever teachings from Jesus are included in the Bible. Lucifer, because he was a God-created Soul of Light, acted as a double agent working both for the Light and the dark side which was his mission.

When Lucifer wanted to include some of Jesus' real teachings in the Bible, Constantine became very suspicious of him. In order to give himself credibility, he told Constantine that the Bible had to be believable otherwise they would not be able to gain the attention of humanity and it would not have the effect intended. "What a brilliant idea," Constantine thought.

Jesus came to teach the Love of God/Creator and that through our connection with Him and receiving His Love and Light, we would free ourselves of the many causes of suffering we were experiencing. Jesus claims that he did not come as a Savior. He came to Earth to show us the way to God through the vibration of Love. He did not have the power to take our sins away. Only we have the power to save ourselves. If He did have that power, we would not be going through the pain and suffering we have been during the last 2,000 plus years.

The Vatican is at the top of the organizational chain of the Illuminati. The Catholic Church used to be one of the most powerful institutions on Earth. This appears to be coming to an end under the direction of Pope Francis I, who is destined to bring about change for the good of the organization.

Jesus believed in the freedom of every human having the ability to communicate with God directly. This is why both the Jews and the Romans were suspicious of Him and felt He was a threat to their teachings and so He had to be eliminated. It appears that the Dark Forces were eliminating individuals who opposed them (including Jesus) over 2,000 years ago, and as I write I am being told this was taking place long before Jesus' incarnation. Therefore, it is now time "we" put a stop to it.

The crucifixion of Jesus was only one possibility in His Life Plan. This outcome could have been altered if enough individuals supported His teachings. He was considered a radical agitator. Again, from the human perspective, Jesus was a complete success. However, from a spiritual perspective, the outcome of His mission was not as expected. Ultimately it was the Dark Forces that made him a success by establishing a religion based on only a small fraction of His purpose for coming to Earth.

Much of the information contained in the Bible has

been manipulated or intentionally distorted to serve those in power and to help them remain in power. Many have turned away from the traditional, fundamental religions for a variety of reasons. However, I believe it was the Awakening Process that caused individuals to look for something that made sense.

When I was writing my first book *Creating Heaven on Earth: A Guide to Personal Ascension* and the information came forward through Jesus that we (humanity) are Gods in training, I struggled with that idea. My problem was that every religion in the world preached that there is only ONE God, so it was not easy for me to switch my belief that I was in training to become a God. However, I knew it was Jesus who was providing that information and while I trusted Him, I wasn't sure the readers would trust/believe me. Those who were at a level of "knowing" the truth had no problem taking in and digesting that fact. It is a reward we earn as a result of the growth achieved during our Earthly incarnations.

MATERIALISM/GREED

Once the Dark Ones had control of our spiritual aspect, next they introduced commerce and industry and the dream of wealth and power. Humanity was turning responsibility over to others and began to judge another's worth by the wealth and power they accumulated. This is how the different classes/castes were created – wealthy/middle-class/poor!

Their purpose was to cause separation not only from God, but from each other. Materialism and greed would eventually cause jealousy, competition, and tension with our neighbors, co-workers, friends, and family. Money or material "things" do not create happiness; they seem to create stress in keeping up with the Joneses.

According to my spiritual guidance, Communism was originally a "good" thing as all citizens were to be provided for equally. However, the Dark Ones turned it into a way of controlling the people so the good intentions were overshadowed by the Dark Cabal.

All of this is part of the evolutionary process and while the darkness was quite successful in obtaining control, I believe it is time for the tables to turn and for humanity to experience what we came here to do – Create Peace and Heaven on Earth! We can do it. I KNOW we can.

PART V

DEPOPULATION

Chapter 16

DEPOPULATION

According to the powers-that-be there are too many of us (humans) – 7.5 billion people. It is getting harder and harder for them to control us. Therefore, a plan of depopulation was created and it includes reduction through natural disasters, famine, pestilence, and biological warfare. This plan was called the "Global 2000 Project."

The necessity for depopulation stems from the few elite from the Secret Societies to be able to maintain control. By reducing the population significantly would make control much easier for them.

Why should the majority of humanity be eliminated just to make things easier for the Dark Ones to control us? I say it is time to stand up and speak up and take our control back. It is time for the Dark Cabal to have the experience of being controlled. One thing you can count on is that they will not like the reverse position at all.

NEW WORLD ORDER (WORLD DOMINATION)

The Illuminati/Dark Cabal's main goal is to create a New World Order (One World Government) where they are in control of all of humanity and humanity would become a slave society. Our only purpose would be to serve the wealthy. There would be only two classes of humans – the wealthy and the workers. The middle class would be eliminated altogether. From where I sit it appears that this is already happening without our knowing it. It would be a good reason NOT to reincarnate to Earth if this does happen.

Their mission is to bring the developed countries, such as the United States and Europe, to a lower standard of living and to bring the standard of living in the third world countries up a notch or two in order to even things out. This will make it much easier for them to manage us if everything is equal.

This mission has been planned in secrecy and kept from the general public through the many different Secret Societies. The members of these Secret Societies have assisted the Illuminati in carrying out their every wish. If they do succeed in achieving a One World Government, I wonder if they will eliminate those who helped them with their mission as they will no longer have a purpose. Just a thought! It seems to be the way they operate.

It is not just the rich and famous celebrities and those in positions of authority who are at risk of elimination. Unfortunately, the majority of humanity is at risk because of the Global 2000 Project. The individuals who are in control seem to have little or no respect for human life.

It is within their capability to control hundreds of millions of humans, but much more difficult to try and control 7.5 billion. Another problem is that we are depleting the resources on Earth. Therefore their solution to this problem is to reduce the number of humans on Earth. It appears that so far that is the only area they have not been able to control – population!

METHODS OF DEPOPULATION

The elimination of certain individuals who go against the "Plan" is not a depopulation effort. It is a "control" effort. The depopulation efforts are two-fold:

1. A slow kill effort through our food, water, air, drugs, illnesses.
2. Massive elimination through wars, weather technology, and frequency technology.

A few of their attempts are listed below:

Prescription Drugs/Vaccinations

Bacteria/Virus/Infections

Chemtrails

Nuclear War – World War III

Nanotechnology Frequency

Mind Control/Brainwashing Techniques

Weather Control Technology

PRESCRIPTION DRUGS

While sometimes these drugs seem like a god-send, if they give us a quick fix, however, most of the time they do more harm than good. If you read the side effects, these drugs cause other problems with our physical bodies requiring yet additional prescriptions to ease the side effects.

VACCINES

Another way to get toxic chemicals into our body legally is through vaccines. Vaccines are designed as a slow kill for humans even though we are told they are intended to protect individuals from a possible deadly virus. Could it be possible that the shingles virus, which appears in old age, is a slow surfacing effect of the vaccine given for chicken pox earlier in life?

A secondary gain in reducing the population is that certain vaccines may cause infertility.

Back in the days of Atlantis, when the Anunnaki were in charge, they introduced a lab-created parasite life form to be implanted at birth or early infancy. These parasites grow claw-type tentacles that travel through the brain, nervous system, and entire body causing all kinds of physical and mental ailments to the human. The purpose for this type of immunization was a dark one – to keep humanity at a lower vibration, sick, and easier to control.

While this immunization was created during the days of Atlantis, it may still exist in today's world. If so, it has to be stopped.

What can we do? Stop feeding the pharmaceutical companies, and paying high prices for their so-called legal drugs. When you read all the side effects including possible death from taking certain drugs, they should be declared illegal.

BACTERIA/VIRUS/INFECTIONS

The goal is to weaken our immune system and they accomplish this by creating viruses such as AIDS, SARS, various annual flus, and a variety of different cancers.

We are kept in sickness and poverty (or as close to it as possible) while the elite get richer and richer at our expense. Greed is the name of their game. However, keep in mind that we "allowed" it to happen and we have the right and the power to change things in our favor.

CHEMTRAILS

Chemtrails are a form of darkness – survival of the fittest. The Dark Ones who are controlling life on Earth are spraying a deadly/toxic chemical mixture of mercury, aluminum, and barium, which on a long-term basis is designed to affect all areas of life through the air we breathe, the water we drink, and the food we eat. These chemicals will have an effect on our health through every one of our body systems, our memory, emotions, and relationships. It is a lethal attempt to reduce the population.

Chemtrails have a dual purpose: 1) speed up the depopulation process and 2) create profits from prescription drugs and possibly other medical services.

It is too difficult for them to control 7.5 billion people. Five hundred million would be much easier. It appears to be a case of survival of the fittest.

Since the information about the chemtrails has leaked to the public through the Internet, I believe this activity has slowed, if not stopped altogether.

FOOD & WATER POISONING

In addition to the chemtrails, our water supply has been poisoned for years through the mandatory additive fluoride. This is unfit for human consumption, but by law it is mandatory in most states to be added to our water supplies.

The chemical additives, such as aspartame, included in our food items and approved by our government are a source of slow death. Aspartame has been known to cause symptoms which mimic multiple sclerosis. MS cannot be cured. However, if the symptoms are caused by aspartame, they can be cleared once you stop consumption of the food items which contain aspartame.

WARS

The Dark Ones create conflict, add fuel to already burning fires by providing misinformation to the two opposing nations; then fund and arm both sides of the conflict. War creates death, but wars also create massive wealth for the already rich through their efforts as defense contractors.

The leaders of our world declare war, make it seem an honorable thing for both men and women to fight for the freedom and rights of the people in our and other countries, when the real reason for war is to obtain world power, control, and more importantly, depopulation.

A statement made by Henry Kissinger to Alexander Haig (White House Chief of Staff) in 1973: *"Military men are dumb, stupid animals to be used as pawns for foreign policy."* I think Henry Kissinger should have been a little more respectful, but it is an example of those working under the umbrella of darkness only being interested in fulfilling their own agenda.

World War III was part of the plan in order to significantly reduce the population on Earth. Fortunately, since the time for darkness on Earth is over, we are assured by the Light powers-that-be that a third world war will NOT happen.

NANOTECHNOLOGY

A frequency of energy aimed to disrupt our vibration and cause many different ailments such as headaches, depression, insomnia, heart attacks, and attacks on our nervous system.

The Dark Cabal used a very high-powered, sophisticated frequency weapon which has the potential to not only kill the human body, but the Soul as well. Soul energy is Source energy and no one has the right to destroy this energy. It can only be transformed from negative (dark) to Light or from Light to dark.

Once the Dark Forces were informed that their reign on Earth had ended, this was a last effort on their part to be victorious. Fortunately, their effort failed as the Light Beings stepped in with healing energy to offset the damage done to the humans who were targeted – the highest vibrational level of Light Beings on Earth.

On a lesser scale, the Dark Forces also used a level of frequency which targeted the heart and nervous systems of Light workers in an attempt to bring us down either through death of a heart attack or through severe pain such as the sciatic nerve renders.

MIND CONTROL/BRAINWASHING/PROGRAMMING

These methods are done through the media as well as mind control programs by the CIA and FBI.

Many of the school shootings we experienced in the U.S. have been done by individuals who are under mind control for the purpose of taking attention away from other acts by the Dark Cabal and shift our attention to more of an emotional agenda. We are considered "fools" by the Dark Ones as we get so emotional about death. To them death is a "blessing."

PROJECT MONARCH

Project Monarch is a CIA brainwashing project which targets young Hollywood celebrities and programs them for success in order to have complete control and absolute power over them. When they step out of line and don't want to be controlled any longer, they are usually blacklisted, discredited or could ultimately experience death such as Robin Williams, Michael Jackson, John Lennon, and a host of others.

WEATHER CONTROL TECHNOLOGIES

Weather control technology was created to cause a small storm to manifest into a severe destructive force, causing much loss of life and property. Humanity is none the wiser. These situations are usually called "Acts of God," meaning that humans had no control so they cannot be held responsible, and the insurance companies usually do not pay for "Acts of God." However, many times it is humans who are causing these storms through experimenting with weather technology.

HIGH FREQUENCY ACTIVE AURORAL RESEARCH PROGRAM (HAARP)

The official facility for HAARP is funded by the U.S. Air Force and is located in Gakona, Alaska. Its mission is highly secret, of course. However it has developed weapons of mind, and mood control in order to cause people to feel depressed, which would have an effect on their behavior.

HAARP weapons can also cause natural disasters, such as earthquakes, hurricanes, tornados, and thunderstorms. Hurricanes Katrina and Sandy were a result of this research depopulation effort.

GMOS – GENETICALLY MODIFIED ORGANISMS

Natural nutrients necessary for a healthy body are removed and harmful chemicals are added. After World War II the Food & Drug Administration was put in place for our protection. Now many highly-placed FDA employees have worked for chemical companies. They should be fired. Something needs to happen.

CLOTHING

Toxic chemicals are prevalent in the manufacture of clothing. They are covered in formaldehyde as a measure to keep them from wrinkling. Then the containers used for shipping are treated for insects with other chemicals. If these garments are worn prior to washing or cleaning, these chemicals are very toxic to the skin.

INVENTIONS

Those who come up with inventions to help humanity such as a very inexpensive source of fuel for the automobile, a cure for cancer, free energy, etc., etc., and make the mistake of submitting their idea to obtain a patent or trademark, the ideas are either denied or bought and then shelved or destroyed. If the original inventor does not concede, it is a very real possibility they will find themselves on the other side through a very natural form of death.

WHAT CAN WE DO TO HELP OURSELVES?

"You must be the change you want to be in the world" – Mahatma Gandhi.

SPIRITUAL AWAKENING/ASCENSION

One thing the Dark Ones put a great effort in was trying to suppress our spiritual growth. Once we reach the Awakening and Ascension levels, they would lose control. As we awaken to what is going on around us, it is not so easy to fool us into going along with their plans for world control and domination. Therefore, depopulation is not going to be the answer to their problem.

Other things we can do to protect ourselves is to boost our immune systems, exercise regularly, and drink plenty of pure fresh water. Do what we can to improve our health. Detox, alkalize. Disease cannot survive in an alkalized, detoxified body.

There are many other methods being used to bring us down – through food additives, genetically modified and processed foods, prescription drugs, plus much more. It is definitely worth whatever effort we can make to lead a life free of unnatural elements.

RX FOR A HEALTHY BODY

The alternative/natural methods of healing what ails you would be a better choice.

Proper nutrition is the best medicine to keep the body in a healthy state. Okay to step off the healthy wagon for a treat occasionally, but should not become the norm.

Proper exercise will also assist the body to stay on the healthy path as will drinking pure water, and getting a good night's sleep. This has always been what is necessary to maintain a healthy body, but we have gotten so used to indulging in the fast and processed foods. Again, occasionally this would do no harm, but a steady diet is what will get us in trouble.

HERBAL MEDICINE

The Food & Drug Administration along with the medical and pharmaceutical corporations are not too fond of herbal-type medicines. And that is because they cannot patent these products and make a huge profit from prescribing them. Restrictions are placed on those who do manufacture and distribute herbal products that they cannot be marketed as a cure for any medical condition. They can only be promoted as a diet supplement.

When God created the human body, he also created the Plant Kingdom as our medicine cabinet. The Plant Kingdom carries the blueprint of the human body and therefore, a variety of different fruits and vegetables provide the body with whatever vitamins, minerals, and nutrients it requires.

So why are these organizations so "afraid" of herbal medicine? It is because it might "cure" what ails us at a very low cost and huge profits would be lost from prescription drugs. In the world of medicine they do not like the word "cure." It is impossible to cure anything, or so they say. There have been many times during my lifetime where I received emails from individuals asking that we write our

Congressmen in order to stop a bill from being passed that would prohibit the use of herbal medicines.

If the researchers were looking out for our health and welfare, they would be spending most of their time and budget finding natural ways of healing instead of combining chemicals that will cause other health issues. The reason the word "cure" is banned, is because, if the doctors and medicines are able to cure what ails us, the profits would dwindle to nothing. There is no incentive on their part to bring us medicines that will CURE anything.

Knowledge is power and we can take our power back by making sure we live a long, happy, and healthy life by eating foods that will nourish us. Our bodies "know" what's good for them and if we pay attention to the signals we receive when we eat something that is NOT healthy, we can significantly reduce any discomfort, and our bodies will serve us better.

PART VI

ASSISTANCE FROM ABOVE

Chapter 17

THE GALACTIC FEDERATION OF LIGHT

Membership is made up of approximately 200,000 star systems within our galaxy which follow the path of Light. Many of the Dark Forces within the galaxy have "crossed" over and joined the forces of Light once they realized that Light was not harmful as they had been told by their leaders.

The Galactic Federation of Light represents many planets, galaxies, and universes in working together for harmonious life for all beings. It is a very large and powerful federation devoted to Universal Love, Light, Peace, and Prosperity.

It consists of hundreds of thousands of members. It is

the oldest federation in the Milky Way Galaxy, founded approximately 4.5 million years ago in order to prevent inter-dimensional Dark Forces from dominating and exploiting the Milky Way Galaxy. The members of the Galactic Federation of Light are loving, peaceful, highly intelligent, and spiritually evolved Beings of Light. We do not have to fear them.

It is important to note that the efforts of the Dark Ones are being thwarted by the Galactic Federation of Light, The Great White Brotherhood, and many other groups of Light Beings not only from our Galaxy/Universe, but from other Universes as well.

The reason they are coming forward in full force now is because the reign of darkness for Earth has ended. It is now time for Ascension, not only for humanity, but for Earth as well. Another reason is that, vibrationally speaking, what happens on Earth affects all the Planets in the Milky Way Galaxy.

Spirit is now able to help us in a massive way. Below they have explained some of the ways they are helping humanity:

- ***Chemtrails*** – *Since this activity would have been very detrimental to the entire planet, we used our power of Light to surround the chemicals as they were being sprayed and transformed them from a deadly state to a neutral state. The Light acted as a transformer of the deadly chemicals rendering them harmless.*

- ***Banking System Fraud*** *– There has been much going on behind the scenes regarding the global financial systems, which has not been reported by the news media. The systems are being restored to a more favorable situation for the majority of humanity. Prosperity will be distributed in the near future as a right you are entitled to. Funds have been stolen from citizens of all countries and unreasonable interest and add-on fees have been assessed in order to keep the populace restricted financially and the Dark Cabal's coffers full.*

- ***Nanotechnology Frequency Weapons*** *– Again the darkness has come up with a solution to the problem of nuclear war weapons being neutralized by using high frequency technology. It is not as harmful for the majority of humanity or Earth itself, but it can be deadly to individual humans. For the most part, it is not fatal to the ones who have been targeted, but it does bring their energy down to a lower vibration.*

- ***Download of Light*** *– In order to accelerate the spiritual growth of humanity there has been a download of Light for the purpose of raising the darkness within each human so that it could be released. Allow it to be dissolved. (When something of a negative nature surfaces, instead of reacting through anger, rage, or any other negative emotion, just let it go).*

- ***Protection*** *– We are doing our very best to protect humans, especially the Light workers, during this time of* *transition from darkness to Light on Earth, as many do not think or remember to protect themselves.*

Please know that it is not always possible for us to do so. Therefore, we recommend that each individual reach up and request protection during this very tumultuous time on Earth as the darkness is able to sneak in and bring very high level Light workers down. This has happened more often than not now that the Dark Ones have been given notice that their time for operating under the umbrella of darkness is done.

Again, we suggest that even though your Guides are doing their best to protect you, it would be helpful if each individual could ask for protection on a daily basis. It is an easy and inexpensive way to ensure not only physical, but spiritual well-being.

- ***Escorting Dark Ones from the Planet*** *– Recently the Light Beings informed the Dark Ones who operate on Planet Earth that their time was up. For them the Great Experiment was over and they had two choices:*
  1. *Return to the Light from whence they came OR*
  2. *Be dissolved as Soul energy.*

  Most have been escorted off the Planet, but there are a few still hiding out. They fear being dissolved (killed) so they are hiding out in humans who have decided upon the path of Light.

I had a client who attracted one of the Grey Reptilians. It caused quite a bit of havoc in their life and this individual spent thousands of dollars trying to be free of this entity.

The Arcturians were able to release this entity and return it to the place where it was created (not of this world).

- ***Working with Light Workers** – who have Soul Contracts to be "whistle blowers." Revealing the wrongs that have been perpetuated against humanity for far too long. Unfortunately, when you are making your contracts on the other side, you agree to bring the darkness to Light during your journey on Earth. However, many times the consequences of your actions would be too difficult for you to accept so you renege on fulfilling that portion of your contract.*

I know I didn't want to write this book once I learned that very special individuals were being killed for similar revelations. However, I have been given assurances by Mother Mary and Jesus/Sananda that I am protected. So the fear I once felt is no longer part of my experience.

> *The Beings of Light are helping all on Earth destined for Ascension during this lifetime. Even if you are preparing for Ascension, but it is not scheduled to happen in this lifetime, we are willing to do whatever we can to assist you in reaching the highest level of vibration possible.*

- ***Clearing Up Pollution** – We have assisted in cleaning up massive pollution in certain areas of the world. One example was the Gulf Coast oil spill. Eventually we will be able to assist in clearing all areas of pollution.*

- ***Mitigating Radiation** – This was possible with the radiation emitted from the nuclear crisis in Japan.*

- ***Oxygen Levels*** – *We assist in keeping your air oxygen levels up to par.*
- ***Eliminating Diseases*** – *More and more individuals are overcoming some of the fatal diseases, and we are happy to assist with this process.*
- ***Natural Disasters*** – *We assist in minimizing, as much as possible, the effects from natural disasters whether or not they are man-made.*
- ***Preventing Nuclear Attacks/War*** – *We have been able to neutralize the nuclear weapons to render them useless in case they are used for any purpose, but specifically for depopulation purposes.*

You might be surprised to know that China, Russia, India and a few other countries are allies of the Galactic Federation of Light and are doing their part in averting the agenda of the Illuminati/Dark Cabal for a New World Order.

Also of interest is a plan for Russia to bring the U.S. down to our knees through frequency technology, not nuclear warfare. It would render us powerless, leaving us in darkness and silence. So I imagine that their plan calls for hitting our electrical grid.

Not sure if the Beings of Light will be able to help us with this situation should it come about, because it is not directed at the world – only the United States. We can lessen the effect this type of attack would have on us by reaching up and asking for help in advance – just to be on the safe side.

CLOUD-SHIPS

Cloud-ships are spaceships camouflaged within a cloud.

I witnessed several during my visits to Mt. Shasta, CA when I attended Dr. Joshua David Stone's Wesak Festivals. During breaks, those of us who would go outside for a breath of fresh air, many times would see above the location where the conference was taking place, disc-shaped objects in the sky, but camouflaged within a cloud. It was the first time I had witnessed anything like that, but it seemed that others from the area were very familiar with seeing the cloud-ships.

I also witnessed one in New Hampshire while out for a drive with my husband. He is definitely a non-believer in space ships, but had to admit that is what it looked like. It was a perfectly beautiful sunny day, blue sky without a cloud in sight when suddenly right in front of us appeared a white cloud that looked like someone had frosted a space ship with a smooth white substance. It stayed for a while and then disappeared.

GALACTIC SHIPS TO THE RESCUE

Right now there are literally millions of Galactic ships surrounding Earth in order to bring the tumultuous end of the cycle of duality to a peaceful conclusion. They are divided into three layers – the largest in the outer layers as these ships are as large as a planet. For the time being, they are out of sight for our protection.

However, the Galactic Federation of Light space ships will appear on Earth when the time is divinely right. For them to do so sooner would be a disaster for humanity. There are many who still carry the fear vibration regarding space ships. Be patient, for we are in good hands if the Galactic Federation of Light is overseeing the dissolution of darkness on Earth.

We (humanity) are Light Beings in the process of waking up from the illusion that has been inflicted upon us from the Dark Ones. The Light Beings are our insurance policy that Ascension of both Earth and humanity will take place as this is the Source/Creator's Plan.

Chapter 18

THE GREAT WHITE BROTHERHOOD

The Great White Brotherhood is a group of supernatural beings of great Light and power who spread spiritual teachings through selected humans. Members are Masters of Ancient Wisdom or Ascended Masters.

Their main purpose for Planet Earth is to work with individuals who are ready to connect with, not only their God Self, but other Beings of Light in order to become empowered. To help these individuals find the truth about themselves and what their purpose is.

Many members of the Great White Brotherhood are in physical form on Earth as it is such a crucial time in Earth's history. They are here to assist us in bringing Light to the Planet and are disguised as normal everyday humans. I have had the pleasure of meeting and working with some of them and it is truly an honor.

EARTH ONCE A CONDEMNED PLANET

At the time when it was decided that Earth would have to be dissolved due to its heavy darkness and lack of Love, Ascended Master Sanat Kumara requested of the Council of One Hundred and Forty-Four to be allowed to go to Earth in an attempt to bring awareness of God's Love to the hearts of humanity. Permission was granted and so he and 144,000 other souls from Venus were commissioned to Earth.

The spiritual being that we know today as Gautama Buddha was one of the first souls to accompany Sanat Kumara to Earth.

Unfortunately, many of these Souls from Venus were not strong enough to resist the darkness and therefore, got caught up in the negativity of Earth and created Karma. It was then decided that humanity needed a great deal of help from the Light Beings in order to reach the level of Ascension rather than dissolve the Planet.

All of humanity has the ability to reach up and connect and communicate with these Ascended Masters at any time during our journey on Earth. They are high vibrational loving beings anxious to help humanity in any way they can.

Following is a message received from Sanat Kumara (a member of the Great White Brotherhood) as I was writing this section:

We would like humanity to know that in order to keep Planet Earth going with the Great Experiment the Source/ Creator had in mind has not been an easy task. At several points in time, Lemuria one and Atlantis two, it was very close to being shut down – dissolved.

However, this would have been a great tragedy for the humans who so willingly took on their assignments. It would have meant failure to a very important mission. Fortunately, the Creator/Source did not want His children to continue to suffer and sink deeper and deeper into darkness. That was not the purpose of the Great Experiment – to punish Souls for there was no reason for punishment.

What is happening now on Earth is the transition phase from dark to Light. While life on Earth is still not what you would call "easy street," it has gotten better, and it will continue to feel better as the Dark Ones recede from their selfish, greedy acts against humanity. It is truly considered inhumane what has been inflicted upon the majority of humanity with no hope for you to survive if things continued as they were.

Therefore, Father & Mother God made the decision that enough time had passed for the darkness to have control of Earth and Humanity. The Dark ETs were NOT part of the original Plan for Earth. It was the Free Will humans had that created the opportunity for the Dark Ones to come forward with the Plan of Domination and Control of not only the planet, but of its occupants as well. Humanity would not have appreciated the outcome of their destiny if Mother & Father God had not put an expiration date on the Great Experiment.

It is time now for humans to experience Peace and Heaven on Earth. You all deserve to have the experience of fulfilling the mission you have suffered for so long. It is your connection with Source/Creator/God and the entire Company of Heaven that will create the heavenly existence on Earth as you have experienced here in the Heavenly Realm.

We appreciate your efforts, and remain in loving service to you for as long as you shall live.

Sanat Kumara

Your Loving and Loyal Servant

8/10/15

It is very appropriate for you to call upon the Great White Brotherhood for assistance. You may even be a member of this Brotherhood. During meditation ask your Spiritual Guides to check the Akashic Records to see whether you are a member. Many humans are members.

Chapter 19

THE ARCTURIANS

The prophet, Edgar Cayce, was the first to make reference to the Arcturians "Arcturus is the highest civilization in our Galaxy."

The Arcturians are guardians of Earth and have been for quite some time. There is no need to be afraid of them for they are very loving and caring and only wish to help humanity on our journey to Ascension. They are highly advanced both technologically and spiritually and God has commissioned them to help humanity in any way they can.

I have had three different references regarding the Arcturians:

- First from Dr. Joshua David Stone while attending his Wesak Festivals in Mt. Shasta, California, and reading several of his books on Ascension.
- Second from Norma J. Milanovich's book *We The Arcturians.* I had met her at one of the Wesak

Festivals and purchased her book. I couldn't put it down. It was absolutely fascinating.

- Third from my own spiritual guidance, who suggested I call upon the Arcturians when I was suffering so much from rheumatoid arthritis. The Arcturians are wonderful healers commissioned by God to help humanity at this time with all the health issues we are dealing with.

Also Sananda and Archangel Michael asked that I call upon the Arcturians to assist me with my Soul Releasement work, especially with the dark entities who did not want to leave.

In my research regarding the Arcturians, I found two different opinions as to where they originated.

1. One was a blue planet near the star Arcturus, which has not been identified as yet. In Edgar Cayce's readings, he mentioned that the Arcturians were from a place near the Star Arcturus so this made sense.

2. The other was that they originated from the star Arcturus.

What I usually do in situations like this is I meditate and call upon the Beings of Light, in this case the Arcturians, and ask which of the two opinions was correct. To my surprise, they are both correct.

Their explanation was that their existence mimicked that of Earth. We are humans on Earth, but when we evolve to higher vibrational levels, we go to a place in the higher dimensions called "Heaven." The Arcturians have growth experiences on the "unknown" blue planet and when they evolve to higher spiritual levels they are assigned to the Star Arcturus, which would be equal to our Heaven.

Right now the help we are receiving on Earth is from the Arcturians who reside on the Star Arcturus, not the blue "unknown" planet. This is similar to the help we are receiving from non-physical Light Beings such as the Archangels, Jesus/Sananda and other Ascended Masters.

I can't encourage you strongly enough to call upon the Arcturians for assistance with any health issues you may be experiencing. I have had tremendous success working with the Arcturians. Due to our Free Will contract, they cannot just step in and "fix" us unless we ask for their help.

I was suffering from an attack of my sciatic nerve. I was using Bengay and aspirin to relieve the pain, when the Arcturians signaled me with goose bumps and asked if I wanted their help in healing. They told me the healing would not be instantaneous, but to be patient. I was and in approximately 6 weeks the condition was completely cleared up without needing any medication/pain relievers.

You may wonder why, if we have all this help available to us, are we in such a DARK state? The answer is simple. The Beings of Light follow the rules of the contract of The Great Earth Experiment. The Dark Ones do not follow the rules and use the most gruesome methods possible in order to be able to take control of humanity and Earth for their own self-serving purposes. If the time for darkness did not end, we would be in a sorry state for sure.

Finally, I have received the following message from the Arcturians:

We, the Arcturians, wish to call forward anyone who would like to use our services for, not only healing, but anything else that they require help with. We are more than willing to be of service to humanity during this time of Ascension on Earth.

It is a wonderful time to be a human and to be able to see the results of the many lifetimes that have led you to this time of Ascension. It is not that other planets have not ascended before as most have. However, it is the first time that one has had the mission of bringing Heaven and Earth together as one unit.

In the future you will be able to visit Earth from the higher non-physical dimensions just as if you were taking a trip somewhere in the physical world. At first it will appear to you as your science fiction movies have been created, but it will not be science fiction – it will be your reality!

We are so excited for humanity to reach the very special time of your creation. We are watching over you as a mother watches over her children. It is our pleasure to be of service to humanity and we bid you good day! We look forward to our continued association with you.

The Arcturians

8/21/15

PART VII

MESSAGES FROM THE HEAVENLY HELPERS

Chapter 20

MESSAGES FROM THE HEAVENLY HELPERS

I had been given a lot of guidance from my wonderful Heavenly Helpers during the process of piecing this book together. Many had told me they wanted to include their message and some gave me more than one message. You will find many other messages included throughout the book where I felt it appropriate to include them. There were a few surprises as well, but what a delight to have had the experience of connecting with all of them. I am listing them in chronological order as received.

The first one came from Samuel (a prophet from the Bible). Due to loss of power from a winter snow storm, I was not able to use my computer, so I sat at my kitchen table with paper and pen, and the following message was received from Samuel on January 17, 2015:

SAMUEL

First of all, darkness is a positive from our perspective here in the Heavenly Realm. It serves a purpose and that purpose is to allow humanity to make choices (called Free Will).

The Creator wanted to see how Souls would react to something which was the opposite of what they were experiencing in the higher dimensions. It truly was an Experiment. Most individuals feel that God KNOWS everything. However, God obtains his knowledge through experiments. It is one thing to assume that under certain circumstances a Soul would react in a pre-programmed way, but given Free Will they may not react as anticipated.

It was thought that if a planet was created at the lower dimensions and it was up to humanity to bring it into the higher dimensions, this Experiment would be referred to as "Creating Heaven on Earth."

There were many setbacks on this road to Heaven on Earth, but at this time in Earth's history, we see that it is a very real possibility that will occur. It is taking the Awakening Process combined with the Ascension Process to get Earth into the higher dimensions.

Earth will evolve into the Seventh Dimension before it will explode and become a star. It will take some time before this happens, but to us in the higher dimensions, it is a success story that we were doubtful, at one point, that it would be a success.

We admire and applaud those who have done their job in bringing this Experiment to a successful outcome. While you do not see it as successful just yet, we are more in a position to see the future and what we see is "SUCCESS" – a complete success. So do not be discouraged and do not give up. We congratulate humanity NOW!!!

Samuel
1/17/15

SANAT KUMARA

Following is a message received from Sanat Kumara on May 4, 2015, at the Cathedral Rock Vortex in Sedona, Arizona:

This vortex was named Cathedral Rock as the rock image resembles a church. This vortex carries a great deal of energy as it is an area where many Light Beings from several different Universes congregate to have meetings. As they meet, their energy replenishes the energy which has been depleted by visitors who do not honor the sacredness of the area.

God has created several such vortexes throughout the entire Planet. However, Mt. Shasta and Sedona are only two in the United States. There are vortexes which have not been discovered as yet on the Planet, but they will be unveiled within the next 50 to 100 years.

Take from this vortex your connection with Sanat Kumara. We have not met yet even though you have heard of me through Dr. Joshua David Stone. I was aware that you were present at his conferences, but you did not know that I would be one of the Light Beings helping you to write your book on the subject of darkness.

It is important for humans to know that they need not be afraid of darkness, but they need to embrace it with the Love vibration. As you know, darkness is simply the absence of Light. Love is Light so why not add Light to the darkness, no matter what form of darkness it is, in order to dissolve it and allow it to experience the difference between its existence as darkness and the experience of Light.

It is really a very simple thing to do, however, it does take patience, determination and persistence in order to win the battle with darkness vs. Light.

It is written in the PLAN that Light shall win when the time is Divinely right and that time is NOW! So, once again, I say "be at peace and you shall overcome Darkness."

With a Great Amount of Respect & Admiration,
I AM Sanat Kumara!

DR. JOSHUA DAVID STONE

Dr. Stone was the one who introduced me to the Ascension Process. I was guided to his books long before I was ready for them. However, once I read his information two or three times I finally got it. I thank him for all the guidance that he provided not only in his books, but during the Wesak Festivals he held in Mt. Shasta, California.

Again, while I was on vacation in Sedona, Arizona on May 7, 2015, Joshua came forward with the following message:

Darkness is something that we see from this side as muck. A lower vibrating energy that is not comfortable to be in or around. Those who feel comfortable in the dark energies are those who have known little of Light or Light experiences.

We had hoped that, once they became of age or were open to make Free Will decisions that they would change what they experienced when others were controlling them, but unfortunately many chose to follow the path of what they had learned from their authority examples.

However, it is destined that Heaven will be brought to Earth and, therefore, the majority rule factor is now in place on Earth.

There are so many more humans who are awakening than there are those who choose to stay stuck and this is meaningful in that humanity will succeed with their mission. It may take a little longer than originally thought, but it DEFINITELY will happen. We give credit to those humans who are willing to step up and take responsibility for the mission they have chosen to do while on Earth.

My experience of being on Earth and following my mission was not an easy one. However, once I tapped into Source energy in order to assist me along my path, everything became much easier.

You, too, have learned this very valuable lesson of allowing spiritual guidance to assist (not control) your actions, and life does become much easier to go through.

This is my prayer for all of humanity that they learn to connect with their own guidance from above and move forward with the greatest of Grace. Blessings to mankind! We await the completion of your mission.

Dr. Joshua David Stone

SERAPIS BEY
MAY 4, 2015

I received two separate messages from Serapis Bey – one on May 4, 2015 while in Sedona, Arizona, and the other on May 19, 2015 while on a Caribbean cruise.

Message received at Cathedra Rock Vortex in Sedona, Arizona:

This is Serapis Bey. I am one of your Guides with respect to the book you will write on the subject of darkness.

We believe that humanity's time has come to see the darkness as an obsolete tool in which to navigate through life. It is time to bring peace on Earth and that can be done through being kind to all humans no matter what station in life they happen to be in at this time.

I have come to you for an introduction and to let you know that I will be connecting with you from time to time with quotes for your book. We appreciate your willingness to present this material to your fellow humans.

Know that you are blessed and that you have many admirers and supporters on this side so do not feel that anything will be able to harm you or your loved ones.

Serapis Bey

MAY 19, 2015

Message received while on a Caribbean cruise:

This is Serapis Bey again. I come to you with a message of HOPE – a message of FAITH.

The darkness which once controlled the Planet Earth is

slowly but surely dying out. The Company of Heaven is doing all that is allowed by spiritual law to help humanity fight the battle. Light has already won. However, the darkness is not fully aware of this fact at this time.

They are starting to "wake up" that there is no leader for them to follow any more so they are on their own. Most of the dark followers are not comfortable with following their own lead and, therefore, are not sure which way to turn.

These are the entities who are now deciding to turn to the Light as an alternative source. They are finding it quite fascinating as they realize that they have been misled by the dark authorities in believing that the Light would "kill" them. They are finding that is not true and that they feel so much better with the vibration of Love (positive) instead of all the qualities that represent darkness – the opposite of Light. They are happy to be rescued and are very sorry when they see in their Life Review that they have harmed individuals needlessly. They are able to feel how they made these individuals feel and it doesn't "feel" good.

This is the culmination of God's Plan for Planet Earth – for those who choose the dark path to awaken and find the Light and KNOW the truth that the Light will definitely set them free from the darkness which they have surrounded themselves in for many, many centuries.

God will be victorious with this Experiment He has chosen for humanity. Humanity will be the next generation of Gods – developing new planets, galaxies, universes.

It will be necessary to create some new Souls in order to occupy these planets, galaxies, universes. So those who are in human form now will be able to view their evolution and decide what these newly created Souls are to experience while occupying their newly created places. There are an infinite number of possibilities.

Some have already had thoughts of what they would create if and when they become a God. Many humans feel it is not right to think of them self as becoming a God for they have been told that there is only ONE God. That is not true.

There is only ONE Source/Creator who initiated all of this. However, Source/Creator needed help in the creation process so IT made possible the opportunity for Souls to be able to climb to higher spiritual levels, and to share in the process of creation.

The Source/Creator does not have ego, so is more than willing to share creation with any Soul who rises to a high enough level to be able to create what is worthwhile for all. Remember even though humanity is having an individual experience, we are all ONE!

We would like to share with your readers that they should start planning/thinking if they were told today to create the perfect Universe, what would they include in their Universe? This is definitely food for thought, but it is not science fiction. It will soon become your reality.

God Bless Each and Every One of You
Serapis Bey
5/19/15

KUTHUMI

Again, I received the following message from Master Kuthumi while on a Caribbean cruise on May 22, 2015:

This is Kuthumi. Greetings to you this morning for a wonderful sunny day. I am here to provide my quote for your book on darkness.

First of all, darkness in not a bad thing. It is only a learning experience. Once you know how to follow your feelings and what feels good is good for you, then life becomes much easier – does it not?

So when humans decide to only go with their good feelings and not to follow their fears, they will have learned the secret to life. That secret is to follow their inner instincts, their heart, their all-knowing self. Life becomes easier and less cumbersome for those who learn that the positive emotions/experiences will lead them to the Light and the negative emotions/experiences will lead them deeper into darkness.

They will truly know the meaning to life. It is when one enters the vibration of the Ascended Master (Fifth Dimension) that this knowledge is realized. All of humanity will reach this point at some time during their lifetime and this is when individual humans will become one in their thought process and then God's Plan will become reality on Earth.

We see, from this side, that many, many humans are working diligently on the Plan in order to bring it about for the masses.

No one human can force another human to awaken or to

ascend. However, the many humans who are reaching the level of Ascended Master for themselves will eventually have an effect on the whole. It is through association with those who are still residing in the Third Dimension mentality that will cause the masses to awaken and ascend in their own time.

Remember, I repeat once again – no one human can cause the Awakening/Ascension for another. They can only lead by their example.

Humanity is in a better position now than ever before in Earth's history to reach its intended goal of Creating Heaven on Earth. It almost seems impossible. However, when the mission for Earth is complete, those who have had an important role in bringing it to fruition will marvel at a job well done!

Life on Earth appears to be a complicated challenge. We agree that it does appear this way when you do not have the knowledge to know the "simple" truth of how to deal with life's challenges.

When you are an infant or young child you look to your parents or other adults to protect and guide you through the challenges that you face on a daily basis, whether that challenge is a bruise due to a fall or a perceived threat which is not real. This is the human way.

The spiritual way is for humans to reach up to Father God for assistance when things become too challenging or overwhelming. Once humans learn to reach up to Father God, their troubles will be dissolved such as a parent kissing a "boo boo" will take away the pain from a child's hurt.

God loves all of humanity – even those who have chosen the dark experience. For God perceives them as just that – an experience. Experiences are meant for growth purposes. The darker the experience one overcomes, the greater their growth. Keep this in mind as you go through life and become enmeshed in the negative experiences.

The more experiences you have and dwell upon them the more they multiply – both positive and negative. Therefore, the best thing to do is recognize that which you do not want, embrace it with Love and send it away. In this way, you will not have to keep re-experiencing the same negative experiences over and over again. You will be able to attract more positive experiences into your life.

This is Kuthumi and I wish you Good Day!
May 22, 2015

MOTHER GOD

I had attended a flute concert by a new friend of mine, David Young, on Saturday evening, June 13 at a friend's home. His music is absolutely magical as it is spiritual in nature. He had given me a copy of a new CD (*Songs From The Higher Consciousness*) he was going to post to his website as a free download in honor of his 25th anniversary of creating spiritual music.

I put his CD on to listen to while I was at the computer working on this book. Much to my honor and amazement, a message came through from Mother God. I asked if she was the Mother God of my Higher Self and she said "No." Then I asked if she was the Mother God who was responsible for Planet Earth and she said "No." She proceeded to say that she was the Universal Mother God who oversees the activities of the universe in which Earth is an occupant, along with Father God.

I had never channeled that high of a vibration before and I attributed it to listening to David's music.

Following is the message I received from the Universal Mother God on June 14, 2015:

Be at peace and KNOW that no matter how things "appear" to be, all is well in your world. The Universe is working to "right" itself and, believe it or not, much is happening behind the scenes in the higher dimensions that will benefit Earth in the future.

We cannot do it ourselves. We need your help in creating

balance on Earth. If each human would right whatever feels wrong within them, then progress will be achieved much sooner. If you think you cannot do anything about what is going on in your governments, think again. If individuals stand up and speak out for what they believe needs to be changed, you will be doing what is right for you. Not everyone will feel the same, but if you do not voice your opinions, they will not be heard.

Hold your head up high during times of defeat. If you have been experiencing challenging times, you are definitely not alone. And you should see improvement soon if you have not already experienced the benefits which we have been showering upon humanity.

Within the next few years on Earth there will be many changes taking place and they will NOT be Earth changes, they will be people changes – changes in attitude, changes in how humans treat each other with Compassion, Kindness, and Love. You will think you have stepped into another dimension, but you will still be on Earth, but a much better Earth than you have ever experienced in any other lifetime.

So, my children, do not allow the darkness to get you down for you are so much stronger and mightier as a Light Human Being than the darkness could ever possess. Move forward along your path and lend a helping hand to anyone who may need it. If you cannot do anything yourself, seek help from others who are in a position to be able to help. It is human helping human where the greatest spiritual growth is achieved.

This is Mother God. On behalf of Father God and myself,

we want you to know that we love you and have not forsaken you.

We are with you, and we are asking you to now participate actively in your role of bringing Heaven to Earth through your thoughts, words, actions, and feelings. We love you and will not allow the darkness to destroy any one of you.

Mother God

6/14/15

PRESIDENT JOHN F. KENNEDY

Message from President John F. Kennedy
10 am – Saturday, July 11, 2015

This morning in my home office, I was reviewing my book material and trying to organize it into sections and chapters when I received massive goose bumps – a sign that someone from Spirit wants to communicate. My first question is always "Are you from the Light?" The response I received was *"Yes!"* I then asked *"What can I do for you?"* and the response was: *"It's not what you can do for me; it's what I can do for you!"* It was the voice of President John F. Kennedy. He had come forward with a message for this book, which is as follows:

First of all my assassination was an opportunity for me to return to the higher realms and prepare for yet another lifetime of trying to expose the Dark Cabal to the people. While the Illuminati operates worldwide, they are now losing ground fast as the Beings of Light are stopping them at every pass where they can hurt humanity.

While I was planning a life in physical form, I was approached by the Galactic Federation of Light and asked if I would be willing to work with them from the realm of Light to fight the darkness. I readily agreed and that is what I have been doing since my passing in 1963. I/We can give the citizens of the United States assurances that it will not be brought down by the darkness. We are able to see what their plans are and the time is now Divinely right for us to be able to intervene on behalf of all of humanity.

The darkness will NOT win. They will not achieve their goal of a One World Government or a New World Order, whatever they want to call their mission. We can assure you that their mission will not be carried forward. This is the best I can promise for the citizens, not only in the United States, which I love so dearly, but for all of humanity.

I thank you for allowing me to come forward and say what I have as a very important message.

John F. Kennedy

7/11/15

When creating the outline for *Darkness: Where Does It Come From?* Sananda had listed certain individuals who would be coming forward with quotes regarding their passing. President Kennedy was on the list along with Robin Williams, John Lennon, Michael Jackson, and a few others.

Robin had come to me and asked if I would include his story. I had asked John Lennon for his permission and quote and he said that my Guides had already approached him and he had agreed. While Michael Jackson was on the list, I did not have to approach him as he also came to me with the help of my Spirit Guides.

When I thought about meditating and trying to connect with President Kennedy's energy, I chickened out. I thought he would not want to get involved so I crossed him off the list.

Evidently it was meant to be as he came forward on his

own. It is obvious to me that he is at a very high spiritual vibration for two reasons:

1) He is working with the Galactic Federation of Light, and

2) His message was not to explain who was responsible for his death, but to give humanity a message of Light regarding our future on Earth not only in the United States, but worldwide. So I thank him for that.

Again, I thank all the Beings of Light who have provided messages of hope for humanity. We can now move forward with confidence that our circumstances are changing for the better and that we will succeed with our mission of Creating Heaven on Earth.

Amen!

AFTERWORD

I know some of this information is mind-blowing – totally unbelievable. Remember you have Free Will to believe what feels right for you. I did not want to believe much of this at first, however, in order to move forward, I took my head "out of the sand" (as Sananda refers to those of us who turn our heads the other way and don't want to acknowledge the truth of what is going on) and decided that I would follow my contract in getting the word out.

Through working with Spirit on this project, I do not feel fear as to what is going on with the Shadow Government. I feel that the Light Beings are on top of things, but are now asking for our participation in completing our mission.

I had a hard time researching and writing this book. I only hope that you were able to read it with an open mind and know that my intention was NOT to create fear, anger or panic, but to bring awareness that WE (all of humanity) have to do our part in bringing not only Peace, but Heaven to Earth. This is our job and now that the reign of darkness is over, please do not be afraid to speak up when you witness a wrong where our government officials are concerned. They need to stop all of this secrecy and be up front with us, and let us have a say in the decisions they are making on our behalf. Obviously, what they have been doing is not in our highest best interest or for our protection either.

I apologize for focusing on the negative things that are going on behind our backs, but there was no other way of bringing this darkness into the Light but divulging some of the aspects that are quite widely known but no one seems to be doing anything about them. NOW is the time for us to shine our Light on the darkness that exists in our communities.

Keep in mind that Earth's purpose was to house both Light and dark entities for the purpose of growing to higher spiritual levels. It was how we reacted to certain circumstances that determined whether we advanced or regressed. In our lower vibration, we clung to the vibration of fear. Fear is something we created on Earth as it does not exist in the higher dimensions. The vibration of fear hindered our growth for many lifetimes. As Sananda has stated, we (humanity) created fear so we have the same power to dissolve it.

It is no longer necessary to fear anything. Move forward under the umbrella of Light and the darkness will have no choice but to melt away or to join the Light. Once darkness is exposed to the Light, it is able to experience the Love that is associated with the Light vibration and it feels good!

I am happy to report that there are multi-billions of really good Souls here on Earth. The majority of humanity are doing their best to lead a God-loving, honest life. It is only a few hundred individuals who have had a major negative impact on humanity and unfortunately, they happen to be the ones in "charge." I am not sure how or when we are going to take control back, I just know that it is something that we MUST do and SOON!

Fortunately, the decision has been made, as the result of what humanity went through during this Great Experiment, to never allow this type of experience to happen again.

Keep in mind that while the ones who played the role of darkness did an excellent job, the time has come for the ones acting out the role of Light to stand up and be victorious in our role of uniting Heaven and Earth.

As I was researching material for this book, I asked my guidance, "Why me?" as many of us do when we are handed an assignment that is not only uncomfortable, but I felt I was not the best person to write about this subject. I did not receive an answer from my guidance, but continued and tried to do the best I could.

When I received the message from John F. Kennedy, Jr., he indicated that I had been a politician in the past when things weren't so corrupt. While this was a little tidbit more than I was aware of, I was still not satisfied. There had to be more than that. I am aware that when we take on a contract to do something "down here," it is for a "good" reason. So, once again, I reached up to my guidance and insisted (I usually don't get demanding with my guides, but I "knew" there was more to this situation) that they tell me WHY I had agreed to write this book.

The day before I was to send my first draft of the manuscript to the editor, the reason why I had agreed to write this book was revealed to me. In the early 1800's I was a presidential aide. I was aware of some things going on behind the scenes that were not "right" and when I voiced my objections, I was quickly eliminated. Not just fired but shot dead!

Again, be careful of what you ask for. Maybe this assignment of writing about the corruption was the easiest way for me to have a voice rather than getting into politics and actually going through what is going on behind the scenes. I now know why my guides did not answer me when I first asked. I was fearful that what happened to others (Robin Williams, President Kennedy, etc.) might happen to me. There is a sense of relief now that I know. And, I can say, that the answer to my big concern was "No," fear has not reentered my vibration as a result of knowing.

I would like to end with a quote received from Sananda this morning, August 19, 2015 in the peace and quiet of my meditation area in the foothills of the Berkshires:

This is Sananda and I wish to tell all who read this book that I guided the author as to what we, in the higher dimensions, felt was important to include in this book at this time. There is so much more that has not been included, but it is no longer important.

It is now time to move forward, forgive those who were operating in darkness and KNOW that all is well in your world as you keep a positive perspective on whatever is placed before you.

It is time to release any negativity you have accumulated, for you will shine the Light within you by doing so. Negativity is like a lampshade on your Soul – it blocks your Light from shining as brightly as it is capable of doing.

We, in the higher dimensions, are doing our very best to assist you in your mission of bringing Heaven and Earth together as ONE!

God Bless you all and we thank you for your service, not only to God, but to Earth and each other.

Sananda
8/19/15

ABOUT THE AUTHOR

Barbara M. Hardie is the Founder and Director of Angel Connections, established in 1995 in Tolland, Massachusetts. Her mission is to help individuals open their awareness of who they are spiritually, to find inner strength and peace, to attract abundance, release negative energy which causes stress/problems, improve health and relationships, and to improve the quality of life in general through spiritual awareness and the process of Ascension.

She is an Ordained Spiritualist Minister, Certified Spiritual Healer, Medium and Counselor through The National Spiritual Alliance. She lectures on a variety of spiritual topics, channels the Ascended Masters and Archangels, and offers phone or email sessions designed to help individuals reach higher levels of vibration.

Her first book *Creating Heaven on Earth: A Guide to Personal Ascension* received two Finalist Awards, one from Best Books – USA Book News and the other from International Book Awards. Her second book *Soul Releasement: Assisting Souls into the Light* received the Finalist Award from Best Books – USA Book News.

She is a Certified Master Hypnotherapist and received her certification through IACT – International Association of Counselors and Therapists. Barbara Hardie has combined her business experience, hypnotherapy skills, and spiritual awareness in developing the programs offered by Angel Connections.

From October 1997 through January 2007, she organized/sponsored/promoted from one to five Mind-Body-Spirit Expos each year throughout New England and New York which she used as a venue to present information on *Soul Releasement: Assisting Souls into the Light*, as well as *Creating Heaven on Earth: A Guide to Personal Ascension.*

Barbara has lectured on spiritual topics and specifically the information contained in her books for the past 20 years to groups large and small throughout New England – in Massachusetts, Connecticut, Vermont, New Hampshire, Maine, and Rhode Island; as well as in Albany, New York; Allentown, Pennsylvania; West Palm Beach, Florida; Chicago, Illinois; and Bend, Oregon. During 2006, 2007, 2009, 2012, 2013, and 2014, she presented workshops and provided spiritual readings on the Royal Caribbean and Celebrity Cruise Lines to destinations in the Caribbean, Spain, Italy, and France in Europe, as well as Alaska and Hawaii.

Her current book *Darkness: Where Does It Come*

From? was a little more challenging to write as it is a subject she was not that familiar with. However, once she realized that she had a Soul Contract to write such a book and she was assured by her Heavenly Helpers that they would be guiding her along the way, she became more relaxed and now is able to see the darkness from a spiritual (Light) perspective.

Visit *www.angelconnections.com* to learn more about Barbara. If you would like to schedule a private session or have a specific question, please email Barbara at: *bhardiema@aol.com*.

ADDITIONAL OFFERINGS FROM BARBARA M. HARDIE

BOOKS

Darkness: Where Does It Come From? (October 2015)

Soul Releasement: Assisting Souls into the Light (September 2013)

Creating Heaven on Earth: A Guide to Personal Ascension (July 2011)

CDS

Forgiveness Garden explains the importance and benefits of forgiveness and includes a powerful meditation channeled from Jesus in order to be able to forgive those who have hurt you, ask forgiveness of those whom you have hurt, as well as an opportunity to forgive yourself.

Manifesting with the Angels helps you to establish goals and practice reinforcing techniques to attract abundance in all areas of your life. Prosperity is part of our spiritual growth experience. Learn why it is NOT wrong to ASK for money/material things. Participate in a powerful meditation to bring your request to the higher dimensions to release them.

Healing with the Angels explains the components of healing and why some people do NOT heal. How you can determine whether or not a health issue you are experiencing is part of your Soul Contract. Experience two angelic healing meditations: 1) *"Garden of Angels"* and 2) *"Healing with the Arcturians,"* which is a time-released healing process in the Ninth Dimension guided by your Higher Self.

ANGEL READINGS

Allow the Angels and Spirit Guides to help you in knowing and understanding the situations that you are experiencing. Feel free to ask questions about any or all areas of your life (60 or 30 minute phone or email sessions).

SOUL PURPOSE READINGS

Who are you? What are you supposed to be doing? Why are you here? Are you on your spiritual path? At this time many are restless, curious about what they are supposed to be doing. Let your spiritual guidance put you at ease in knowing what your purpose/life mission is for this lifetime (60 or 30 minute phone or email sessions).

The Angel Readings and Soul Purpose Readings can be combined into one session if you prefer.

REMOTE SOUL RELEASEMENT SESSIONS

Soul Attachments – if you think or feel that you have an entity or entities attached to your energy/auric field, Barbara can check to see if this is the case. If so, she can release them and have them escorted to the Light and then cleanse and groom your energy from any residue of negative energy the entity/entities may have left behind. (This session can be done from a distance and is usually done in the early morning hours.)

EARTHBOUND SOULS

If you know of an individual who has passed from physical form to spirit and you believe they have not gone to the Light, Barbara can assist their Soul to their new home on the Other Side. (This work can be done remotely through meditation and connecting with the deceased individual's soul energy.)

RELEASEMENT FROM RESTING AREA

If a loved one has passed and you want to know where they are and if they arrived in the Light, Barbara can check on their whereabouts. If they are in the Resting Area (an area where the Soul goes when they are carrying a lot of negative energy,) Barbara counsels your loved one's Soul until such time as they are ready to be received into the Light.

Visit www.angelconnections.com

Email Barbara at: bhardiema@aol.com to:

Sign Up to Receive Special Messages from Spirit,
Products & Services Offers, and Upcoming Events.

Order additional copies of her books and CDs:

Books:

Darkness: Where Does It Come From,

Soul Releasement: Assisting Souls into the Light

Creating Heaven on Earth: A Guide to Personal Ascension

CDs:

Forgiveness Garden

Manifesting with the Angels

Healing with the Angels.

Schedule private sessions or request pricing.